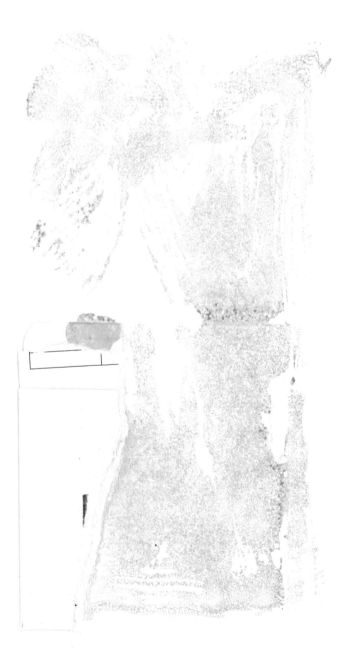

Library Overdues

Analysis, Strategies and Solutions to the Problem

Library Overdues

Analysis, Strategies and Solutions to the Problem

Robert Burgin and Patsy Hansel
Editors

The Haworth Press
New York

Library Overdues: Analysis, Strategies and Solutions to the Problem has also been published as *Library & Archival Security,* Volume 6, Numbers 2/3, Summer/Fall 1984.

The Haworth Press, Inc., 28 East 22 Street, New York, NY 10010

Library of Congress Cataloging in Publication Data
Main entry under title:

Library overdues.

  Includes bibliographical references.
  1. Libraries—Circulation, loans—Addresses, essays, lectures. 2. Library fines and fees—Addresses, essays, lectures. 3. Library rules and regulations—Addresses, essays, lectures. 4. Libraries and readers—Addresses, essays, lectures. I. Burgin, Robert.
Z712.L53 1984 025.6 84-19736
ISBN 0-86656-376-8

Library Overdues:
Analysis, Strategies and Solutions to the Problem

Library & Archival Security
Volume 6, Numbers 2/3

CONTENTS

Introduction

Patsy Hansel
Robert Burgin

The articles gathered here focus on one of librarianship's most persistent, but least effectively discussed, problems—overdues. Not only are statistical analyses and hard data generally lacking in this area; it is also rare that the actual everyday overdues procedures of a library are outlined in the literature.

The editors have attempted to bring together in this volume statistical data on overdues, systematic presentations of overdues procedures from various libraries, a closer look at certain reactions of libraries to the overdues problem—legal proceedings, automation, fines—and a consideration of the theory behind many of our overdues practices.

The lead article, "More Hard Facts on Overdues," is based on two surveys (1981, 1983) of public libraries, and sets the stage statistically for the articles that follow. The authors attempt to give the overdues problem a more rigorous treatment than they have been able to find previously in the library literature. The goal of the surveys was to determine what tactics employed by libraries in their battles against overdues could be validated statistically as effective. The survey results indicate that many of the "solutions" libraries employ in an attempt to reduce overdues do not work. However, several activities are revealed to be significantly helpful: restricting patrons with overdue materials, automating circulation, using a collection agency, sending the first notice within 15 days of the due date. Perhaps the authors' most important conclusion, though, is that there are no easy answers to the overdues question. Of course, that is what managers are paid for—to come up with answers for their own libraries to problems whose solutions are not clear-cut.

Patsy Hansel, Assistant Director, Cumberland County Public Library, Fayetteville, NC 28302. Robert Burgin, Associate Director, Forsyth County Public Library, Winston-Salem, NC 27101.

1

The second article highlights the solutions of a particular library—a library judged an outstanding performer from its overdues return rates in the two surveys. The article is a step-by-step description of the library's overdues process with copies of the forms in use. After reviewing statistics and overdues procedures for several years now, the editors believe that the secret of effectiveness in dealing with overdues lies not so much in the discrete tactics a library employs but in the way the total process comes together. Rowan Public Library, the focus of this article, has developed a process that works very well in their local area and which some other systems may choose to emulate.

Kathleen Moeller-Peiffer looks at some alternative approaches to the overdues problem in "Novel Approaches to Overdues, or The Ones Who Borrow and the Ones Who Lend." Tactics such as amnesty days or taking the legal route are still fairly novel, although Moeller-Peiffer points out that they are hardly new.

The legal approach to the overdues problem has received a large share of publicity during the past several years, and the editors have included three articles on the topic. Art Goetz comes down firmly on the get-tough side of the question. He includes a detailed description of the process he follows in Maryland, as well as comments from other librarians who have taken the legal route. Marilyn Murray follows with a summary of the successful procedure that Baltimore County instituted in 1983. Included are the forms used by that library in the procedure. "Three Libraries and Overdues Law" summarizes the experiences of three more public libraries with the legal system, as well as copies of various forms and the statutes under which each library operates. What comes through clearly in all of the articles devoted to the use of the legal system is that the library must work closely with the people who operate within the court system to make sure that library staff know the rules of the court system and follow them to the letter and that library record keeping must be flawless if it is to stand up to the scrutiny of the court.

Although the treatment of the overdues problems of *public* libraries has received the most attention in the library press, other types of libraries have similar problems and are doing their best to come up with effective solutions. Jean Walter Farrington presents the academic perspective in "Overdues and Academic Libraries: Matters of Access and Circulation Control." An academic library's various groups of users require different approaches to encourage

0

Patsy Hansel and Robert Burgin

them to return books, says the author, who then offers some suggestions on how to go about it. "Outfoxing Overdues in the Hospital Library" is a light-hearted approach to the overdues problem in a small special library. In this sort of setting, tactics can change to fit even the idiosyncracies of individual patrons. "Managing Overdues in the School Library" is a detailed description of one school library's overdues procedure, which includes the use of a microcomputer to generate notices.

Automation, micro or otherwise, promises to deliver a measure of relief to the tedium of manual overdues procedures. Willie Nelms details the application of a microcomputer in a public library to supplement the manual procedures in the overdues process. "Library Automation and Overdues: A Description of Possibilities and Potentialities" provides a general outline of how automated circulation systems handle overdues and presents considerations from an overdues standpoint to keep in mind when selecting an automated system.

Two articles follow and deal with the philosophical questions inherent in libraries' approaches to the problems of overdues. "The Fines—No Fines Debate" highlights the pros and cons of that most prevalent method of encouraging the return of materials, the fine. Barbara Anderson then looks beyond the question of our responses to overdues to ask how those responses affect what the public thinks of us. In "Overdues and the Library's Image," the author suggests that fines and other strict measures associated with overdues might be worse than ineffective: they might contribute to a negative image of our institution.

The volume concludes with a bibliography by Terry Bossley which lists over fifty articles from the library literature (dating from 1889) which deal with various aspects of the overdues problem. The editors hope that the bringing together of these citations will aid efforts in research of this age-old problem.

Likewise, the editors hope that the articles in this volume will help librarians develop a more systematic and effective approach to dealing with overdues.

More Hard Facts on Overdues

Robert Burgin
Patsy Hansel

ABSTRACT. A survey of public libraries from across the United States was conducted in 1983 to determine the relationship between overdues and activities designed to combat the problem. Several activities were significantly effective—restricting patrons with overdue materials, automating circulation, using a collection agency, and sending the first notice within 15 days of the due date. While many other activities are not effective, it is helpful to know that such activities can be abandoned without adversely affecting overdues rates. Trade-offs and implications for library management are discussed.

In 1981, a group of librarians in North Carolina became frustrated enough with the absence of "hard" data on overdues to do something about it. They surveyed librarians throughout the state to find out what the overdues picture was really like, they sponsored two workshops to bring librarians together to discuss the survey's findings, and they published the results of the survey.[1]

The 1981 survey posed more questions than it provided answers, but it did identify some tendencies and some statistically significant factors in the overdues process.[2] Most significant was the correlation between a library's overdues rate—the percentage of books due for a given time period that are still overdue—and the population served by that library. Libraries with larger service populations had significantly higher overdues rates in the long run, i.e., one, two, and three years after the books were due.

A second significant factor was the time at which first notices were sent out by a library. Libraries that sent out notices within two weeks of materials being overdue reduced overdues rates by a sta-

Robert Burgin, Associate Director, Forsyth County Public Library, Winston-Salem, NC 27101. Patsy Hansel, Assistant Director, Cumberland County Public Library, Fayetteville, NC 28302.

tistically significant margin in the short run (overdues rate for the latest due date) and in the very long run (three years after the books were originally due). In addition, those libraries with the expeditious first notice tended to have lower rates for one and two years after the books were due.

A third significant factor was the loan period. Again, over the very long run of three years, libraries which had loan periods of 28 or more days significantly outperformed libraries with loan periods of medium length, 17 to 21 days. The longer loan periods tended to yield lower overdues rates across the board.

In addition to the few significant findings, there were some tendencies—not statistically significant, but tendencies nonetheless. Some made sense. Some did not; for example, libraries that restricted patrons with overdues by not letting them borrow more books had higher overdues rates.

The fact that no tendencies or significant differences were found for some factors was itself an important finding. For example, there was no significant connection between fines and overdues rates. Libraries that charged fines tended to have better return rates in the short run, but over the long run, libraries that did not charge fines got slightly more books back.

In essence, what the 1981 survey found was that few of the activities that librarians engaged in were effective in lowering the percentage of books that would be overdue.

THE 1983 SURVEY

The authors conducted a follow-up survey in the fall of 1983. The follow-up survey was conducted not only to attempt to confirm the findings of the original survey but also to expand the survey to include libraries from across the nation and to change the time intervals for which overdues data were gathered.

In addition to the 70 public library systems in North Carolina, 81 public libraries from outside the state were chosen at random from the *American Library Directory*. By the time compilation of data had begun, 89 surveys had been returned. Thirty-six of the surveys came from libraries outside North Carolina; fifty-three from North Carolina libraries. (The North Carolina surveys represented 43 public library systems. Some systems returned a survey form for each member library.) The overall response rate was 79 of 151 public library systems, or 52.3 percent.

The 1981 survey had calculated overdues rates for four time periods: the last due date; 1980-81 (i.e., materials checked out one year prior to completion of the survey); 1979-80; and 1978-79. Since the overdues rate dropped most dramatically from the last due date (an average of 17.14 percent in the 1981 survey) to the one-year mark (.74 percent) and since the rate after the first year fell very little (from .74 percent to .63 for two years and .56 for three years), the authors decided to look at time periods within that first year to see if overdues and circulation activities might be more effective earlier in the overdues process. Consequently, the 1983 survey form asked librarians to provide data for the last due date, for a date six weeks prior to completion of the survey, for a date eight weeks prior, for a date four months prior, and for a period of time one year prior to completion of the survey. Thus the survey provided data for two periods of time identical to those of the first survey (last date and one year prior) and for three new periods of time.

Again, the effectiveness of circulation and overdues activities was determined by using the *overdues rate*, the percentage of a library's circulation for a certain time period that was still overdue when the survey was completed. The rates for libraries engaged in certain activities were compared with the rates for libraries not engaged in those activities. Overdues rates were compared for significant differences based on a t-test, with .05 as the level of significance. If libraries engaged in a particular activity had significantly lower overdues rates than other libraries, that activity would be considered effective in reducing overdues. Where applicable, library characteristics were compared with overdues rates to determine correlation based on a Pearson r, with the level of significance again set at .05.

RESULTS

Tables 1 through 18 summarize the findings of the 1983 survey. Table 1 shows the mean overdues rate for all responding libraries for the five time periods. For the most recent due date, 13.95 percent of books checked out were still overdue—almost one book in seven. For books due six weeks earlier, the overdues rate dropped to 3.78 percent—one book in twenty-six. For books due eight weeks earlier, the overdues rate was 3.00 percent; four months earlier,

2.78 percent. For books due one year earlier, the overdues rate was 1.15 percent.

Compared with the 1981 survey, the overdues rate for the last due date was lower (13.95 percent in 1983, 17.14 percent in 1981) but not significantly so. The overdues rate after one year, however, was higher in the 1983 survey (1.15 percent versus .74 percent in 1981) but, again, not significantly so. There were also no significant differences between the mean overdues rates for North Carolina public libraries and those for libraries outside the state. (See Table 2.)

Much of the 1983 data tended to confirm that of 1981. As in the 1981 survey, the data in 1983 showed a tendency for those libraries not charging fines to have a better overdues rate in the long term but a more difficult time getting books back on time. (See Table 3.) However, the no-fines libraries came closer to the fines-charging libraries in getting books back at the due date than they had in the 1981 survey. (In 1983, the fines-charging libraries had a mean overdues rate of 13.91 percent for the last due date; the no-fines libraries had a mean of 14.21 percent in 1981. In 1981, the gap was larger— 16.52 percent for libraries charging fines; 26.81 percent for those not charging fines.) The 1983 results did indicate that if a library is going to charge fines, it ought to charge stiff fines. The survey found that the amount of the fine had a significant negative correlation with the overdues rate for the last due date. In other words, the higher the daily fine, the faster the books came back. (See Table 18.) However, for the respondents to this survey, the highest fine charged was a rather paltry 10 cents a day. Ten of the libraries charged that amount; 58 charged 5 cents or less. Although not on the questionnaire as such, the authors were interested in determining whether a library's fine structure made a difference in its overdues rate. That is, would a complex structure of fines (for example, different fines for adult books, for children's books, for new books, and the like) cause items to be returned any more expeditiously than would a simple, one-fine-for-every-item procedure? The data showed no significant difference. (See Table 4.)

In the 1981 survey, libraries not allowing patrons with overdues to check out more materials tended not to get more books back. The 1983 data, however, showed that restricting patrons with overdues was the only factor to prove significant at every interval; at every interval, libraries that restricted overdue patrons did significantly better at getting materials returned. (See Table 5.)

In the 1981 survey, "shorter and longer loan periods tended to

Table 1

Mean Overdues Rate

(Number of Libraries Responding in Parentheses)

	Last Date	6 Weeks	8 Weeks	4 Months	1 Year
Rate	13.95 (81)	3.78 (75)	3.00 (73)	2.78 (71)	1.15 (61)

Table 2

Effect of Library's State

	Last Date	6 Weeks	8 Weeks	4 Months	1 Year
North Carolina	12.82 (52)	3.62 (50)	2.99 (48)	2.75 (46)	1.20 (35)
Non-N.C.	15.99 (29)	4.10 (25)	3.02 (25)	2.84 (25)	1.08 (26)

Table 3

Effect of Charging Fines

	Last Date	6 Weeks	8 Weeks	4 Months	1 Year
Don't Charge	14.21 (7)	7.36 (6)**	2.86 (7)	4.63 (7)	.86 (7)
Charge Fines	13.91 (73)	3.50 (68)**	3.06 (65)	2.62 (63)	1.21 (53)

**Significant difference, .05 level

Table 4

Effect of Fines Structure

	Last Date	6 Weeks	8 Weeks	4 Months	1 Year
Simple	14.16 (46)	3.95 (44)	3.47 (42)	2.71 (42)	1.29 (31)
Complicated	13.12 (25)	2.77 (22)	2.51 (21)	2.57 (20)	1.18 (20)

Table 5

Effect of Restricting
Borrowing Privileges of Patrons with Overdues

	Last Date	6 Weeks	8 Weeks	4 Months	1 Year
Restrict	13.25 (61)**	2.74 (55)**	2.27 (53)**	2.21 (51)**	.82 (48)**
Don't Restrict	16.30 (16)**	6.79 (16)**	5.65 (16)**	4.40 (16)**	2.97 (10)**

**Significant difference, .05 level

produce lower. . .overdues rates across the board.''[3] The 1983 results continued to support this finding. (See Table 6.) Both shorter—14 days or fewer—and longer—28 days or more—loan periods proved significantly more effective at four months. Libraries with longer loan periods did better by a significant margin at the last due date and at eight weeks. By one year after the due date, however, the longer period's advantage had disappeared, but there was still a tendency for the shorter period to produce lower overdues rates.

As in 1981, libraries that renewed books had worse rates than those that did not, at the last due date. (See Table 7.) But in the 1983 survey, the difference was significant. That difference, however, disappeared by eight weeks and actually reversed itself, though not significantly.

As in 1981, libraries that sent the first overdues notice out quickly (within 15 days) did better than the rest. (See Table 8.) The advantage was significant at six weeks but diminished after that. Those that sent four or more notices tended to do better, significantly so at six weeks; and if the final notice was a bill, the library tended to get more books back, significantly so at six weeks, eight weeks, and four months. (See Tables 9 and 10.) Although only a few libraries charged fines by the notice as opposed to by the item, those that did were more successful than those that did not, significantly so at the

Table 6

Effect of Loan Period

	Last Date	6 Weeks	8 Weeks	4 Months	1 Year
10-14 Days	15.00 (28)	3.32 (25)	2.41 (25)	1.84 (25)**	.52 (21)
20-24.5 Days	14.88 (39)**	4.44 (37)	4.00 (34)**	3.94 (32)**	1.49 (26)
28+ Days	9.29 (14)**	2.79 (13)	1.62 (14)**	1.80 (14)**	1.49 (14)

**Significant difference, .05 level

Table 7

Effect of Renewing Books

	Last Date	6 Weeks	8 Weeks	4 Months	1 Year
Renew	14.22 (75)**	3.86 (70)	2.96 (68)	2.76 (66)	1.12 (58)
Don't Renew	10.64 (6)**	2.65 (5)	3.46 (5)	3.09 (5)	1.74 (3)

**Significant difference, .05 level

Table 8

Effect of Sending the First Notice
within 15 Days of Material Being Due

	Last Date	6 Weeks	8 Weeks	4 Months	1 Year
Sent in 15 Days	13.89 (39)**	3.39 (36)**	2.99 (34)	2.77 (33)	1.27 (29)
Not	16.18 (20)**	6.11 (19)**	2.49 (18)	3.01 (18)	1.37 (19)

** Significant difference, .05 level

Table 9

Effect of Sending 4 or More Notices

	Last Date	6 Weeks	8 Weeks	4 Months	1 Year
Send 4+	12.57 (2)	.55 (2)**	1.26 (2)	1.44 (2)	.51 (2)
Don't	13.92 (69)	4.05 (64)**	2.81 (62)	3.03 (60)	1.21 (54)

**Significant difference, .05 level

Table 10

Effect of Making the Final Notice a Bill

	Last Date	6 Weeks	8 Weeks	4 Months	1 Year
Final is Bill	13.31 (42)	2.81 (40)**	1.99 (38)**	1.87 (38)**	.97 (36)
Is not	14.65 (39)	4.90 (35)**	4.09 (35)**	3.83 (33)**	1.42 (25)

**Significant difference, .05 level

Table 11

Effect of Charging per Notice

	Last Date	6 Weeks	8 Weeks	4 Months	1 Year
Charge Per Notice	11.66(9)**	1.92 (9)**	1.95 (9)	3.27 (8)	.53 (8)
Don't	14.29(70)**	4.08 (64)**	3.15 (62)	2.69 (61)	1.25 (52)

**Significant difference, .05 level

last date and at six weeks. (See Table 11.) Calling overdue patrons proved to be unproductive. As a matter of fact, at eight weeks, libraries that did *not* call got significantly more books back. (See Table 12.)

Although the 1981 data showed that libraries that took tardy patrons to court had significantly higher overdues rates, this finding

Table 12

Effect of Telephoning

	Last Date	6 Weeks	8 Weeks	4 Months	1 Year
Telephone	14.44 (45)	4.35 (41)	3.89 (41)**	3.13 (40)	.78 (31)
Don't	13.63 (34)	3.12 (32)	1.83 (30)**	2.44 (29)	1.57 (29)

**Significant difference, .05 level

did not hold in the 1983 results. (See Table 13.)[4] Those few libraries that used a collection agency did get more books back, significantly so at the last due date. (See Table 14.)

In 1981, libraries serving larger populations had significantly higher overdues rates in the long term. As in 1981, the 1983 data showed population to be a significant factor after one year. (See Table 18.) Unlike the 1983 study, though, the larger libraries had better return rates at the last date. In fact, those over 100,000 population served had significantly better rates at the last due date than those under that figure. (See Table 15.) By the end of the first year, however, the smaller libraries did quite a bit better. There was also a positive correlation between overdues rates and the number of staff devoted solely to overdues; in other words, the more staff devoted solely to overdues, the higher the overdues rate proved to be. (See Table 18.) A positive correlation began to take hold at eight weeks, but it was not significant until after one year. After eight weeks, libraries with more staff devoted solely to overdues tended to have more overdues, significantly so after one year.[5] There was also a strong correlation between what libraries pay overdues staff and a high overdues rate, which becomes significant at eight weeks. (See Table 18.)[6]

The type of circulation system a library chose did not seem to make a difference in the return of material, unless it was an automated system. Although only four libraries in the sample had automated circulation systems, they did a significantly better job of getting books back when they were due. (See Table 16.)

The authors' favorite statistic was one showing that those libraries that changed something about their overdues procedures after the 1982 overdues workshops mentioned earlier did better across the board than those that did not make such changes.[7] In fact, they performed significantly better at the last date and at four months. (See Table 17.) This finding confirmed our suspicion that the libraries

Table 13

Effect of Taking Patrons
with Overdue Materials to Court

	Last Date	6 Weeks	8 Weeks	4 Months	1 Year
Go to Court	14.85 (13)	3.16 (13)	2.55 (12)	2.95 (11)	1.69 (12)
Don't	13.54 (67)	3.86 (61)	3.07 (60)	2.78 (59)	1.02 (49)

Table 14

Effect of Using a Collection Agency

	Last Date	6 Weeks	8 Weeks	4 Months	1 Year
Use Agency	10.67 (2)**	1.83 (2)	2.37 (2)	2.58 (2)	.18 (1)
Don't	14.04 (79)**	3.84 (73)	3.01 (71)	2.78 (69)	1.17 (60)

**Significant difference, .05 level

Table 15

Effect of Population Served

	Last Date	6 Weeks	8 Weeks	4 Months	1 Year
Under 100,000	15.12 (59)**	3.99 (54)	3.13 (53)	3.00 (51)	.72 (44)
Over 100,000	10.32 (10)**	4.00 (9)	3.58 (8)	3.12 (8)	2.44 (8)

**Significant difference, .05 level

Table 16

Effect of Automating Circulation

	Last Date	6 Weeks	8 Weeks	4 Months	1 Year
Automated	8.72 (4)**	3.50 (1)	3.28 (2)	4.11 (2)	2.51 (2)
Manual	14.23 (77)**	3.79 (74)	2.99 (71)	2.74 (69)	1.11 (59)

**Significant difference, .05 level

Table 17

Effect of Implementing a
Change in Overdue Procedures

	Last Date	6 Weeks	8 Weeks	4 Months	1 Year
Made Change	9.26 (13)**	2.29 (13)	1.42 (11)	1.03 (11)**	.47 (9)
Did not	14.00 (39)**	4.08 (37)	3.46 (37)	3.27 (35)**	1.45 (26)

**Significant difference, .05 level

Table 18

Correlations Between Activities
and Overdues Rates

	Last Date	6 Weeks	8 Weeks	4 Months	1 Year
Fines Per Day	-.3604 (68)**	-.1375 (58)	-.0778 (53)	-.1359 (48)	.1028 (48)
Population	-.0440 (69)	-.0921 (60)	-.1574 (55)	-.1632 (51)	.3286(52)**
FTEs Devoted to Overdues	.1036 (8)	.0972 (9)	.5725 (8)	.5570 (7)	.8487(9)**
Salaries Paid FTEs Devoted Solely to Overdues	.3354 (8)	.6204 (8)	.6762 (8)**	.6834 (6)	.2600 (8)
Prorated Salaries Spent on Overdues	-.0082 (42)	.0306 (39)	-.1341 (35)	-.2376 (34)	.3027 (33)

**Significant, .05 level

that take overdues seriously were the ones that would get their books back.

THEORIES

It is possible to break the various factors into three categories: uncontrollables, reactions, and actions. The uncontrollable factors are those (like population served) that a library cannot control. For example, the 1983 survey found that libraries with populations of 100,000 or more get more books back at the due date than do smaller libraries. That finding is of little consolation to the smaller library. Findings related to these uncontrollable factors may be interesting, but they are not helpful.

Some findings may be categorized as reactions. Libraries that called overdues have higher rates (up to one year, at least) than those that did not. Obviously, calling people did not cause them to keep their books out past the due date. The cause was the overdues rate. That higher rate was "causing" those libraries to resort to calling their patrons. There was a similar conclusion in the earlier study regarding taking people to court. It was intuitively obvious that a policy of taking patrons to court would not "cause" those libraries to have higher overdues rates, that instead the policy had been adopted in response to those libraries' high rates of overdues. Unfortunately, findings in the reaction category offer little in the way of advice and, in fact, may confuse the issue by blurring cause and effect.

Finally, there are actions. For instance, the survey found that if the final notice was a bill, the library sending it tended to get more books back, significantly more at six weeks, eight weeks, and four months. If a library does not already do so, the advice is clear: make the final notice a bill. Findings that certain activities are associated with lower overdues rates are productive. Such findings provide advice to librarians that certain activities should at least be tried.

There is also an implied piece of advice: don't engage in activities that do not have a significant impact on the overdues rates. If an activity like fines does not produce its intended effect—significantly reduced overdues—then the librarian should either abandon the activity as unproductive or seek to justify the activity on other grounds.

In summary, the following activities were found by the survey to be associated with significantly reduced overdues rates for the time intervals listed.

Last Date—Charge 10 cents per day in fines
　　　　　　Restrict patrons with overdues
　　　　　　Automate circulation
　　　　　　Don't renew books
　　　　　　Use a collection agency
　　　　　　Loan books for at least 28 days
　　　　　　Charge fines per overdue notice sent
　　　　　　Send the first notice within 15 days

6 Weeks　—Charge fines
　　　　　　Restrict patrons with overdues
　　　　　　Send four or more notices
　　　　　　Send the first notice within 15 days
　　　　　　Make the final notice a bill

8 Weeks　—Restrict patrons with overdues
　　　　　　Make the final notice a bill
　　　　　　Loan books for at least 28 days

4 Months—Restrict patrons with overdues
　　　　　　Make the final notice a bill
　　　　　　Loan books for at least 28 days or
　　　　　　　loan books for fewer than 15 days

1 Year　　—Restrict patrons with overdues

CONCLUSION

As with the original survey, we are left with more questions than answers. But two things are clear, one discouraging and one quite encouraging.

On a discouraging note, it appears once again that many of the activities in which we engage in an attempt to reduce overdues simply do not work. Additional staff devoted to overdues, fines for overdue materials, complicated fines structures, telephoning patrons with overdue books—none of these traditional "solutions" produced lower overdues rates in the public libraries that we surveyed.

However, it is encouraging that several activities were significantly helpful—restricting patrons with overdue materials, automating circulation, using a collection agency, sending the first notice within 15 days of the due date. It is also helpful to realize that many of the time-consuming activities associated with overdues procedures can be abandoned without an adverse effect on the overdues rate.

There are, of course, trade-offs. By not renewing books, a library may tend to get more overdues back at the due date. But at what cost to the library's image and at what cost to circulation? Or consider the conundrum presented by the findings on the effectiveness of fines. Libraries that charged fines, especially those that charged relatively stiff fines, got more books back at the due date and at six weeks after the due date than did libraries which did not charge fines. However, the libraries that charged no fines outperformed the fines-charging libraries after one year. Is it then more important to get some books back as soon as possible but at the expense of losing a few more in the long run?

These dilemmas point to an important characteristic of management itself. Even the best of surveys on a complex issue such as overdues will not dictate a manager's decision. Surveys can only provide data to help managers make choices or, in some cases, to more clearly delineate what choices there are to make.

REFERENCES

1. Patsy Hansel and Robert Burgin, "Hard Facts About Overdues," *Library Journal* 108 (February 15, 1983):349-352.

2. The authors emphasize that throughout the article, the terms "significant" and "significance" refer to the concept of *statistical* significance, by which we mean that there is

evidence for concluding, with some confidence, that the findings reflect real differences in the survey population and that the findings are not random.

3. Hansel and Burgin, 350.

4. Perhaps by 1983, the option of taking people to court was beginning to make an impact.

5. Since population served correlated with overdues rate at one year and since larger libraries are more apt to have staff devoted to overdues, this may signify a reaction to a problem, as did going to court in the 1981 survey.

6. Again, this may be a reaction to a problem. But it does show that "throwing" staff and money at overdues doesn't do much good.

7. Changes included sending out first notices five days sooner ("with an improved return rate"), calling patrons with overdues ("moderately successful"), using triplicate overdues forms ("a savings in staff time"), writing up overdues after two weeks ("an increase in overdues returned earlier"), using a form for patrons who claim to have returned materials, eliminating second notices ("saves postage"), raising fines from 5¢ to 10¢ per day ("do not have as many overdues now"), automatically renewing items, delaying the sending of overdue notices until items are two months overdue, and taking a "kinder" approach.

"In Search of Excellence": How One Public Library Copes with Overdues

Melody Moxley

ABSTRACT. The author examines the overdues procedures of a medium-sized public library that has been able to greatly reduce its overdues rate. The library sends two notices, gives a six-day grace period in circulated materials, employs one fine slip, and relies on legal action for patrons with over $50 in materials overdue. Sample forms are appended.

(Editor's note: A recent best-seller on management sought lessons on managerial excellence by looking at outstanding companies. Likewise, the following article outlines the overdues procedure for a public library which, based on the 1983 Burgin and Hansel survey, is an outstanding performer in the overdues realm. While the Rowan Public Library has an overdues rate at the last due date (13.50 percent) which is close to the mean for all libraries in the survey (13.95 percent), by eight weeks past the due date, Rowan's overdues rate (.35 percent) is substantially lower than the mean for all libraries surveyed (3.00 percent). At one year, that difference persists (.44 percent to 1.15 percent).

In addition to the information supplied by Ms. Moxley, the following may be gathered from Rowan's annual report to the State Library and from Rowan's survey form. The Rowan Public Library serves a population of 100,230 with a staff of 28.8 FTEs and a 1982-83 operating budget of $572,770. An estimated 23 hours per week of staff time are devoted to overdues, at a cost of approximately $6,090 per year. A 5¢ per day fine is charged on all overdue materials; in 1982-83, total annual income from fines was $6,951.02. The Rowan Public Library circulates books for twenty-one days and renews them, although not by telephone. Rowan uses a Gaylord charging machine for recording circulation transactions.)

Melody Moxley, Rowan Public Library, Salisbury, NC 28144.

19

The Rowan Public Library (of Salisbury, North Carolina) uses a two-notice system. This is the streamlined and simplified version of a system that originally required the sending out of four notices (first, second, and third notices, and then a bill). The present version has, I feel, been streamlined as much as possible, while still enabling the library staff to keep accurate records and remind the patron twice about overdue materials.

The Rowan Public Library gives its patrons a six-day grace period on all materials circulated (with the exception of equipment). Therefore, there is no fine on overdue materials until the seventh day after the due date. Our overdue system takes this into account, as the beginning of the process occurs on the seventh day after the due date (the first day that materials are subject to a fine).

This system employs one fine slip, which serves as a record for all aspects of the procedure, including patron and overdue material information, a record of the date notices were sent (and returned to the library, should this occur), the date material was returned and the fine dues, and the price of the material. (We charge replacement costs for all overdue materials not returned, plus a processing fee.)

One week after material is due, circulation cards are pulled, and a fine slip is written for each item, using only information found on the card (patron's number, item identification, and date due). The slips are filed behind the cards in clear plastic jackets. Two weeks after the material is due, the fine slips are separated from the cards. Patron information is found and recorded on the slip, and a first notice is typed, with the carbon or second copy typed on a bill form and filed, to be sent later if the material has not yet been returned. The fine slips are filed in the patron overdue file. Two weeks after the first notice has been sent out (one month after the item was due), replacement costs (from *Books in Print*, or from our records, if the item is out of print) are determined for all items not returned, a processing fee is added, the information is added to the bill, and the bill is sent to the patron.

A system of clear plastic, color-banded jackets is used in the patron overdue file. The fine slips are filed in the appropriate color jacket, depending upon the stage that has been reached in the procedures. This ensures quick identification of the patron's status by the staff member when the overdues file is consulted, as it is in the case of every patron borrowing materials. Patrons are considered delinquent when they accrue a fine beyond our limit ($2.00 at this time) or when they have been billed for materials and the materials have not been returned. The color-banded jacket system enables the staff to quickly identify patrons as non-delinquent (a first notice has been sent, but not a bill, or the patron has a fine under $2.00) or delinquent. In the latter case, the patron is not allowed to borrow any materials until the materials have been returned or the fine paid.

One month after a patron has been billed for overdue materials with a total in excess of $50.00, the patron is liable for further legal action. The patron is notified that legal action will be taken if the material is not returned. Ample response time is given. If materials are not returned, the case is referred to Small Claims Court or, if the patron no longer lives in the county, the local Credit Bureau.

All cases that we have taken to Small Claims Court have been settled in our favor, with the materials either returned or paid for. We have not received return of all materials or reimbursement for them in every case referred to the Credit Bureau but, as stated above, only the cases of persons who no longer live in Rowan County are referred to the Credit Bureau.

APPENDIX I

ROWAN PUBLIC LIBRARY
OVERDUE PROCEDURES

1. FINE SLIPS—PREPARED MONDAY-FRIDAY

    A. Pull the overdue circulation cards seven (7) days (1 week) after the due date.

    B. Prepare a fine slip for each card, filling in the patron's library card number, DO NOT look up the name and address. Place the fine slip behind the book card, and cover both of these with a clear plastic jacket. Re-file under due date, as usual. (See Figure 1.)

        a. If the book is returned from 7-14 days after it is due, card in the book, enter the date returned and calculate fine on the slip found behind the card, and file the fine slip, with a clear plastic jacket, in the overdue file. (See Figure 2.)

2. FIRST NOTICES—PREPARED MONDAY-FRIDAY

A. Pull the overdue circulation cards fourteen (14) days (2 weeks) after the due date.
B. Separate the cards from the fine slips. Arrange the fine slips in numerical order and look up the patron's name and address for each slip.
C. Type the first notice, using carbon paper and a bill as the second copy. Type the patron's name, address, card number, date the book(s) were due, and the author and title of the book(s). The date the materials were due should be typed above "due date." The billing date, which is

```
Card No.      1939
Name
Address


Call No.      791. 437
Accession No. 76-0506
Author  Harmetz, Jean
Title  The making of the
      Wizard of Oz
Date Due      1/6/84
Date Returned
Fine Due
1st notice sent
Bill sent
Court letter sent
Notice returned
Price of material
Processing fee
Total
Notes
```

FIGURE 1

Card No. _____1939_____
Name_____
Address_____

Call No. ____791. 437____
Accession No. _76- 0566__
Author _Harmetz, Jean__
Title _The making of the_
_____Wizard of Oz_____
Date Due_____1/6/84____
Date Returned _1/20/84___
Fine Due_____.10_____
1st notice sent_____
Bill sent_____
Court letter sent_____
Notice returned_____
Price of material_____
Processing fee_____
Total_____
Notes_____
_____

_____

_____

FIGURE 2

four weeks after the due date, should be typed on the
space labeled "billing date": (See Figure 3.)
D. Separate bills and First notices. Put all bills for that date
together and file in bill box.
E. Mail first notices.
F. Indicate date on which first notice was sent on fine slip;
cover fine slips with green jackets; file in overdue file.

3. BILLS—PREPARED MONDAY-FRIDAY

A. Pull the overdue circulation cards twenty-eight (28) days
(4 weeks) after date due.

ROWAN PUBLIC LIBRARY—HEADQUARTERS
201 W. Fisher St.—P.O. Box 4039
SALISBURY, NORTH CAROLINA 28144
(704) 633-5578

ROWAN PUBLIC LIBRARY—SOUTH BRANCH
102 North Central Avenue
LANDIS, NORTH CAROLINA 28088
(704) 857-3579

TO Margaret Hamilton

39 Kansas Street

Salisbury, NC 28144

BILLING DATE February 6, 1984

LIBRARY CARD # 1939

Please return the following overdue materials: Due January 6, 1984

author   title   due date

Harmetz, Jean The making of the Wizard of Oz

If materials are not returned, a bill to cover replacement costs will be sent on the
above billing date.

Charges for overdue materials are 5¢ per item, per day, not to exceed $2.00 per item.
This fee is used to cover costs of notification.

FIGURE 3

    B. Pull bills filed and typed for that date.
        1. Going to circulation file, pull book cards for the dates being billed. Check these cards against the bills and mark bills for which there are no book cards. These bills will not be sent, as the book(s) have been returned.
    C. With the bills in numerical order, go to the fine slip file and check for a fine slip for each bill.
        1. Pull slips for bills that are to be sent. If no slip is on file for a bill that is to be sent, one should be made.
        2. In the case of bills that are not to be sent, the slip should be previously marked to indicate that the book(s) have been returned; if not, discard the slips.
        3. The absence of a slip for a bill which is not to be sent indicates that these materials have been cleared from the file, and all is well.
    D. When these steps have been taken, the bills which will not be sent should be discarded.
    E. Check the shelves for books to be billed. If not found, calculate prices, add to bill, and mail to patron. (See Figure 4.)
    F. The price of the book(s) should also be noted on the fine slip, along with the date on which the bill was sent. Cover bills with black jackets and file in overdue file.

4. DELINQUENT LETTER

A. A letter warning patron that he/she may be referred to the Credit Bureau or to small claims court will be sent six (6) weeks after due date if the total amount due meets or exceeds existing limit.

5. CALCULATING FINES

A. When a book is returned, the fine should be entered on the slip and the slip re-filed with a clear jacket unless the fine is over $2.00; in that case, the slip should be covered with a red jacket. (See Figure 5.)

B. A red or blue jacket indicates a delinquent patron, and service will be denied that patron until their account is cleared.

6. LOST BOOKS

The charge for lost or badly damaged material will be the price listed in the latest *Books In Print,* plus a processing fee. If the material is not listed in BIP (e.g., recordings, out-of-print books, etc.) then the price noted on the shelflist card, in current catalogs, or other selection aids will be charged. If no

---

ROWAN PUBLIC LIBRARY—HEADQUARTERS
201 W. Fisher St.—P.O. Box 4039
SALISBURY, NORTH CAROLINA 28144
(704) 633-5578

ROWAN PUBLIC LIBRARY—SOUTH BRANCH
102 North Central Avenue
LANDIS, NORTH CAROLINA 28088
(704) 857-3579

BILL TO:__ Margaret Hamilton _____ BILLING DATE_February 6, 1984_
_____39 Kansas Street_____ LIBRARY CARD #___1939_____
_____Salisbury, NC 28144_____

OVERDUE MATERIALS:

_____ Due January 6, 1984 _____
_Harmetz, Jean____ The making of the Wizard of Oz _____
_____ 12.95

PROCESSING CHARGES ___1___ @___1.00____ ..... _____1.00_
_____ @_____ ...... _____
TOTAL DUE... .. __13.95_

These are replacement and processing charges. They will not be imposed if items are returned immediately. However, all items are subject to overdue fines, not to exceed $2.00 per item.

FIGURE 4

Card No. _____ 1939_____
Name _____ Margaret Hamilton_____
Address _____ 39 Kansas St._____
_____ Salisbury, NC 28144_____
Call No. _____ 791.437_____
Accession No. _76 0506_____
Author _Harmetz, Jean_____
Title _The making of the_____
_Wizard of Oz_____
Date Due _____ 1/6/84_____
Date Returned _____
Fine Due _____
1st notice sent _1/20/84_____
Bill sent _____ 2/6/84_____
Court letter sent _____
Notice returned _____
Price of material _____
Processing fee _____
Total _____
Notes _____
_____
_____
_____

FIGURE 5

price can be located, then the following standard fees will be charged.

Book (hardback)	$ 5.00
Book (paperback)	2.00
Record and tape	7.00
8mm or Super 8mm film (silent)	15.00
8mm or Super 8mm film (sound)	35.00
Read-along (with paperback)	7.00
Read-along (with hardback)	10.00
Filmstrip (silent)	10.00
Filmstrip (sound)	15.00
Pamphlet	.50

7. PROCESSING FEE

In addition to the charge assessed for the replacement price of the material, an additional processing charge will be assessed per item. The processing charges will be as follows:

Book (hardbacks and paperbacks) .... $ 1.00
Single record 2.10
Multi-record set 3.20
Cassette 1.65
Other audio-visual material 1.00

It should be emphasized that this additional charge is not a penalty or fine, but represents money that the library spent to select, order, catalog and process that material.

8. WITHDRAWAL OF OVERDUE MATERIAL

When an item has been overdue for two (2) years it will be considered lost and should be withdrawn from the collection.

9. REFUNDS

Refunds will be made for materials which patrons have paid for and subsequently found and returned to the library. A fine of five cents per day (not to exceed the maximum fine of $2.00) will be subtracted from the amount refunded.

Refunds will only be given to patrons who produce a receipt proving that materials have been paid for or when the duplicate can be located in the receipt book.

10. COVERAGE

Overdue fines will not be charged on materials circulated through the bookmobile and outreach due to the special nature of these services.

11. RETURNED NOTICES

A. Locating the Correct Address
   1. Check the registration file to be sure the address was copied correctly.
   2. Check the registration file to see if a newer address is listed on the patron's registration card.

 3. Check the phone book and/or city directory.
 4. Call the patron using the latest phone number listed in the registration file or other source.
 5. Get the address of the company where person is employed and send the notice there.

NOTE: When an updated address is located, be sure to record this information in the registration book.

B. When a New Address is Located
 1. Double check to see if the book has been returned by checking the circulation file.
 2. If the material has NOT been returned
    a. Type up a new notice. Send the 1st Notice by first class mail.
    b. Pull the fine slip from the overdue file.
    c. Record the new information on the fine slip, i.e., the new address, date the notice was returned, the date the new first notice was sent.

C. If the Patron Cannot be Located

 1. Indicate the date the notice was returned on the fine slip.
 2. Write in Red on the top of the fine slip: GET CORRECT ADDRESS
 3. Cover the fine slip with a BLACK banded jacket and file in the overdue file. The patron will be considered delinquent until the address is corrected.

Novel Approaches to Overdues or the Ones Who Borrow and the Ones Who Lend[1]

Kathleen Moeller-Peiffer

ABSTRACT. This article looks at current attempts at dealing with overdues. The most familiar method—overdues fines—has continued to produce a great deal of debate. The use of collection agencies, mailgrams, and legal proceedings is examined, as well as the use of a local Dispute Settlement Center. Other innovations include a "conscience box" for the payment of fines, a "Customer Services Department," and a phone-a-thon. The author then examines how circulation and overdues policies affect the return of materials.

To match a book with a reader, and to circulate that book to the reader, is (to most librarians) a joyful experience. Attempts to retrieve that same piece of material when it becomes overdue can lead even the most enthusiastic of librarians (or library assistants) to frustration (at best) or early retirement (at worst).

The purpose of this article is to acquaint readers with the current methodology, as reported in library literature during the past three years, for dealing with the bane of librarianship—overdue library materials.

In all of the methods of retrieval that will be reviewed, the same goal exists—to prompt the borrower to return the loaned material in order to make it available for future readers. A corollary to this goal is that librarians wish to avoid purchasing replacements, preferring to spend the library budget on new acquisitions.

Kathleen Moeller-Peiffer, Head Librarian, Orange County Public Library, Hillsborough, NC 27278.

29

Before detailing current methodology, it may be interesting to note that libraries of fifty and sixty years ago also had their worries with overdue materials. The Newark (New Jersey) Public Library Trustees declared an "Overdue Book Week" in 1932 because patrons were not using the library due to the fines they had accrued and could not pay, partly because the Depression years had set in.[2] Fines were cancelled, books returned, and a permanent "Conscience Box" was installed outside the library for the return of library materials (the forerunner of the book return unit). "Fine Cancellation Week" was held at the Boston Public Library that same year; all overdue fines were voided if books were returned, and a new library card was issued to delinquent borrowers.[3] In addition to recovering books and re-registering delinquent borrowers, over two thousand non-library users joined the library as patrons. Alternatively, the Providence (Rhode Island) Public Library refused to hold any fine-free days for the reasons that these days were unfair to those who returned materials on time, that they did not reduce or eliminate future overdues, and finally, that most people with overdue materials were not poor and unemployed but able (yet unwilling) to pay their fines.[4]

Does the above sound familiar? If so, it is the author's hope that the following review of methods other librarians have used to encourage the return of overdue library materials may provide you with new ideas to use in your library setting.

OVERDUE FINES

Currently, librarians have devised a great number of methods to retrieve library materials. Overdue fines are probably the most familiar method, yet there is still debate on this issue. Should we eliminate our fines or increase them? Hardly anyone will admit to being satisfied with his or her current fines structure. On the side of fines elimination is Helen Bryant, who feels that overdue fines instill fear of the library, especially in a child.[5] She feels that children will be angry at the librarian for necessitating borrowing money from their parents, and that if social responsibility is a goal, then not allowing the child to check out materials would be a better lesson than fines. Another media center librarian, Carol Truett, reports the following benefits from a no-fines policy: bookkeeping was reduced; rapport with students, parents, and faculty was increased;

students were pleasantly surprised not to be assessed nickels and dimes when returning library material; and losses of circulating library material were cut by 26 to 51 percent.[6]

On the opposite side of the debate are those who run the library as a business. As such, fines and fees make good economic sense. In an editorial in the Fall 1980 issue of *Connecticut Libraries*, Frank Ferro senses the need for fines, but states that they should be termed "overdue charge" or "extended use charge."[7] This change in semantics, he believes, would remove the onus of punishment that surrounds the recovering of a "fine" from the patrons and would help them better understand the reason for the cost.

Mildred Frazier, an Indiana media specialist, takes issue with the view expressed by Ms. Bryant and Ms. Truett.[8] Her experience in a kindergarten-through-sixth-grade environment indicates that a two-year experiment to remove fines resulted in an increase of overdue materials. In addition, teachers requested that fines be reinstated. Their reasoning was that students showed more eagerness to return materials on time when fines were charged. Janice Hankins agrees with this concept; the benefits that she cites in a school setting include teaching responsibility, budgeting (students pay fines from allowances), math (learning how much change is due after a fine is paid), and the "plus" of using fines money to buy new items to be enjoyed by all the students.[9]

The Goodnow Public Library (Sudbury, Massachusetts) reinstated its fines policy after a two-year "no fines" trial.[10] Although the initial goals of decreasing paperwork and money handling and improving public relations were accomplished, negative reaction set in. Materials began to be kept out by patrons for longer periods of time, the paperwork for mailed overdue notices tripled, and patrons were dissatisfied with the percentage of materials that were not available when they were needed (96 percent of materials were returned under the fines policy; this dropped to 80 percent when no fines were charged). In order to "soften the blow" of fines reinstatement, a three-day leniency period was established. From the fourth day on, however, patrons were charged the full fine. In addition, senior citizens were exempt from overdue charges.

A corollary to charging fines is the recording of them. Frank Van Zanten, of Mid-Hudson Library System, recommends a 3″ by 5″ two-part form.[11] One part is kept for library records; the other is given to the patron. The category of "Library Fines" may be changed to "Overdue Processing Fee" or "Donations," the latter category allowing patrons to use their payment as a tax deduction, a wonderful public relations consideration.

Finally, the stiffest fines implementation found in recent literature came from the Chicago Public Library.[12] Under a 1979 law, fines were boosted from a maximum of $10 to $50 to $500 per item.

"Amnesty" or "fines-free" days and weeks have been used to encourage the return of library materials since the early 1930s. First started as a way to alleviate the financial pressures of the Depression years, it has been continued as a publicity mechanism, a means to generate goodwill among library patrons, and of course to have library materials returned to the collection.

Atlanta Public Library held a massive campaign to retrieve overdues in early 1980.[13] McDonald's restaurants cooperated by giving free food coupons to persons returning overdue materials and by acting as a depository for these items. Television and radio spots were run, newspaper ads were placed, and an announcement was made at an Atlanta Braves baseball game. Over twenty-five thousand books, or one-eighth of the library's overdues, were retrieved during this two-day period.

The Metropolitan Washington Council of Governments held a fines-free week in 1980, with over eighteen thousand overdue items returned to the public libraries in the area.[14] Credited with the success was a highly effective, broad-reaching publicity campaign.

"A Fine Idea" was the title of the amnesty project of the San Francisco Public Library in 1980.[15] Over eighteen thousand books were returned, with positive publicity and financial savings accruing to the library. "Feel Fine Free" had been held by the San Francisco Public Library in 1974, and twenty-one thousand items were returned during that drive.

Utilizing a slightly different approach to fines collection is the St. Paul Public Library (Minnesota) and their levying of "service charges." Rather than the more common method of charging fines on a per diem basis, this library has a five-day grace period, after which the service charges increase sequentially: six to fourteen days, 75¢ for adults, 25¢ for children; fourteen to forty-nine days, $1.50 and 50¢ are charged; over fifty days, $5 and $2. This eliminates the need to calculate the exact number of days a book is overdue, resulting in a time savings at the circulation desk. Fines receipts did not change noticeably, and at the time of the article (February 1981) it was too early to know if more books were being returned than under the old daily fines system. One noticeable problem with this method is the possibility that patrons will keep an item out for the maximum number of days overdue (forty-nine days instead of fourteen), thereby lowering the satisfaction rate of patrons needing materials being kept out an additional thirty-five days.

COLLECTION OF CHRONIC OVERDUES

Only one instance of the use of a collection agency to retrieve long-overdue library materials has been cited in recent library literature.[17] The Free Library of Philadelphia instituted this overdues policy in 1982 to recover materials that were overdue at least one hundred days and for which an overdue reminder and a demand bill had already been sent. Over one thousand books were returned during a six-month experiment with the agency; these materials had previously been deemed "hopeless." The collection agency sent a progression of letters to the patron, indicating that a negative credit rating, revocation of credit cards, and the loss of other financial privileges could be the result of non-return of library materials.

A slightly different version of the traditional overdues letter has been used by both the Buffalo and Erie County Public Library and the Knoxville-Knox County Public Library.[18,19] They are sending mailgrams. Buffalo and Erie County recovered almost $2,000 worth of books and materials, and the library hopes in the future to lease a mailgram terminal in order to be able to modify the text of their overdue notices. Knoxville-Knox County also has been pleased with their mailgrams and did install a terminal in the main library. Mailgrams are delivered as the third notice, have greater impact than a letter, and are assured of next-day delivery. Included in the text of the letter is the phrase "within 72 hours we will send a representative to your home for collection." The "representative" is a library employee who makes a personal visit to recover the overdue materials, but who does not collect fines. In one year of home visits, over $12,000 worth of materials were recovered. The only cost to the library is an hourly salary and reimbursement for mileage. This is one of the most unique ideas discovered during a literature survey, and one that could work effectively given the right set of circumstances (a polite library employee, a fairly compact service area, and a nonviolent library patron).

As the dollar amount of overdue materials checked out by a patron increases, so do the attempts to retrieve those materials. The Penrose Public Library (Colorado) has a patron who had 130 library books overdue for almost two years.[20] It is a state law that willfully holding library books more than thirty days past due is a misdemeanor, resulting in incarceration. The library view was that prosecution was necessary because of the amount of materials involved. The article did not mention whether the ultimate goal had been accomplished—return of or reimbursement for the 130 items.

The Chicago Public Library (Illinois) has also instituted the procedure necessary to have arrest warrants served on the worst offenders.[21] The first time this was tried (December 1979), the six persons who were served with warrants had $2,627 in library materials.

In an attempt to mediate disputes prior to turning them over to the legal system, the Orange County Public Library (North Carolina) spoke with their local Dispute Settlement Center. This organization, originally instituted to accept referrals from the court system in order to lessen the "congestion" on the court docket, agreed to handle six cases per quarter for the library. To initiate the process, the librarian selects those cases of overdues that are at least three months overdue, have already received three notices, and have at least $25 worth of material belonging to the library. Those patrons' names and addresses are then turned over to the Dispute Settlement Center staff, who send a letter to the patron. The letter lets the patron know that the library has requested mediation and that ignoring the request could lead to legal action, and a date is established for the session. Prior to the session, the librarian checks the shelves to be sure that the books are still missing and to verify that the book cards show the patron's signature. During the mediation session, two volunteer mediators work with the librarian and the patron. The librarian explains the library's desire to have the material returned or the cost reimbursed, and the patron is free to give an explanation of the overdues. The mediators keep the discussion "on track," and encourage both parties to negotiate for the best possible conclusion. In one case, it was agreed that the patron would return the materials in good condition by a set date and would pay a reduced fine. This was accomplished even though the patron had previously ignored three notices from the library staff. At the end of the session, the mediators make a record of the agreement reached, and a copy is given to each party. The chief benefits of this process are that nonpartisan witnesses are present during the discussion and that the discussion is held in a neutral location for both librarian and patron. During the first two uses of this system, 50 percent of the library's chronic overdues were resolved.

In order to put "teeth" into the enforcement of overdue procedures, librarians may wish to follow the example of Catawba County Public Library (North Carolina). The county commissioners of that library passed a local ordinance regarding the "retention, removal, destruction, etc.," of library materials, making the above crimes a misdemeanor. While the penalties of a $50 fine or thirty days imprisonment may be imposed, the main objective of the ordinance is to let the delinquent borrower know that county government stands behind the library in protecting materials from intentional theft or damage. It has been used in one instance to recover a film valued in the hundreds of dollars.

SMALL CLAIMS COURT

I was unable to find a citation in the literature for libraries using court methods for resolution of overdues; therefore, I will describe briefly my experience with the judicial process.

After three overdue notices and an attempt to mediate the problem through the Dispute Settlement Center, the Orange County Public Library issues a Small Claims Court summons to a selected number of patrons. Since the cost of paperwork and manpower to issue the summons is $19 in each instance, only those patrons whose overdues exceed this figure in cost of replacement to the library are issued a court order. The books and their value are listed on the form provided by the Court, and a representative of the county sheriff's department delivers the summons. A court date is set, at which time a representative of the library is expected to be present.

The results of our first use of this method were as follows: one patron declared that he had returned his materials; two patrons paid for their overdue materials in their entirety; one patron had moved and could not be located. We feel that this is a fruitful method, especially valuable for the fact that it demonstrates to the delinquent borrower that we will pursue return of the library material and to the taxpayer that we are attempting to protect community property.

NEW APPROACHES TO AN OLD PROBLEM

Some of the newest methods for overdues demonstrate considerable innovativeness. Barbara Walker of BHM Regional Library (North Carolina) reports in *Library Administrator's Digest*[22] that she established a "conscience box" for the payment of overdue fines. Rather than using staff time to calculate the exact amount of overdue money owed, she relies on patrons paying whatever amount they feel is suitable. (This same method is frequently used by charitable groups in selling candy for fund-raising efforts.) Ms. Walker reports that she receives more funds than under the old "count-the-number-of-days" method.

As reported by Will Manley in the June 1983 issue of *Wilson Library Bulletin*, sometimes a rethinking of the overdues problem leads to a fresh approach.[23] At the Scottsdale Public Library (Arizona), the staff who handle overdues are called the "Customer Services Department," thereby ridding this work of any predetermined negative label and emulating what has been used in retail business. The other innovative elements include training these staff members in public contact skills, stressing management and diplomacy; letting them have the privacy of an office in which to discuss the situation with the patron; and giving them the responsibility to make decisions according to each person's need. Besides encouraging a more positive and empathetic view of the patron with overdue fines or material, this change in focus helps to alleviate crowding at the circulation desk as well as the embarrassment of being accosted for fines in front of other library patrons.

Among other activities, the Enoch Pratt Public Library (Maryland) held a phone-a-thon in conjunction with the "Bring back the book—make yourself feel good" campaign.[24] Similar to mass telephone calling associated with charitable fund raising, even the Mayor of Baltimore telephoned delinquent patrons to encourage the return of library materials. Thirty-six percent more overdue materials were returned in August, 1982, than in the same month in 1981, including 58 percent of those labeled "unable to collect." Enoch Pratt used another incentive to have library books returned— a $1 discount on tickets to a Baltimore Orioles home baseball game.[25]

Although complete articles could not be found, two methods of dealing with overdues and fines were mentioned in an article by Charlyne Van Oosbree in the May 1980 issue of *Show Me Libraries*.[26] The first states that a delinquent borrowers' list is posted in the library and in the local newspaper as a first notice of overdues, relying on embarrassment as a motivating factor for book return. The second mentions an Iowa Library that allows delinquent borrowers to work off their fines by giving community service to the library, thus averting the situation of a patron who is willing, but unable, to pay fines.

From Australia, librarian Joy Guyatt has used a flow chart to detail the steps involved in the overdue process.[27] Her method for assessing overdue penalties closely resembles the point system currently used in North Carolina's Department of Motor Vehicles to determine driving privileges. In her process, a set number of points is charged for each day an item is overdue. In her academic setting, she follows the following guidelines: under two hundred points per semester—clear record at the end of semester; two to six hundred points—withdraw library privileges for two weeks; six hundred to one thousand points—interviewed by librarian prior to library privileges being restored. The strength of this system is that it frees the librarian from making subjective decisions and enables major offenders to be treated differently from occasional delinquent borrowers.

The foregoing examples clearly demonstrate that the ways in which overdues may be handled by a library are only limited by imagination and, to a lesser extent, staff time available. The following paragraphs list some final areas that are worthwhile considering before revising one's overdue procedures.

First, is the circulation period appropriate to the material and the clientele? Two recent studies[28,29] have indicated that the majority of items are returned to the library four weeks after they have been checked out. Judging from the length of most best sellers (several hundred pages) and from the fact that many people are conditioned to monthly statements in other areas (bills from charge accounts, doctors, etc.), perhaps we should relax our restrictions and follow what seems to be a natural check-out period for our patrons. This would save us the annoyance of trying to retrieve material prior to the four-week cycle, and patrons would be able to adapt it to their schedules (pay bills, return library books, etc.).

Secondly, are evening and weekend hours made available so that employed persons may return their books to the library? If finances prohibit this, is a book return unit provided outside the building? Better yet, are there multiple return units throughout the service area? (Just think how awkward it would be if everyone had to go to the post office to simply mail a letter—how convenient to place mailboxes in malls, downtown shopping areas, and other heavily travelled areas.)

If charging fines is decided upon, is the fines structure such that it will motivate people to return the books on time? The question to ask is: would you care as strongly about returning a book promptly if the fine was 2¢ per day—maximum charge 60¢ per month—or 10¢ per day—maximum charge $3.10 per month? Put another way, would you pay your bills on time if there were no penalty for late payment?

Finally, is there a well-thought-out policy for dealing with serious and chronic offenders (whatever one's definition of this term may be)? If it is known that one can skip paying his or her electric bill and still have electricity, will the bill be paid? Why should people return library books if only one or two feeble attempts are made to obtain their return or reimbursement for them?

A final word of advice: one should do what is right for himself or herself, the library staff and the community. I hope that this article has provided some suggestions towards that goal. Happy Collecting!

ADDENDUM

An overdues survey has recently been conducted by Robert Burgin and Patsy Hansel as a follow-up to their earlier article in *Library Journal*. Regarding novel approaches to overdues, they have shared ideas from their respondents with this author. Ideas not already covered in the preceding article include the following: no fines are charged for books returned on Sunday; an Eagle Scout collected overdue books as a scout project; canned food was given to the Salvation Army in exchange for overdue fines; police officers collected books door-to-door; and a local Boy Scout troop called overdue patrons and collected their books.

REFERENCES

1. L. Harding, "2 races of men [those who borrow and those who lend]," *Ontario Library Review* 66 (June 1982): 8-12.
2. "Newark's overdue book week," *Library Journal* 57 (May 1, 1932): 438.
3. "Fine cancellation week," *More Books* 7 (1932): 340.
4. "Conscience days for public libraries," *Library Journal* 57 (December 1, 1932): 1008.
5. Helen Bryant, "Encourage use, eliminate fines," *Indiana Media Journal* 2 (Winter 1980): 16.
6. Carol Truett, "To fine, or not to fine: one school library's experience," *Top of the News* 37 (Spring 1981): 277-280.
7. Frank Ferro. "Fees for extended use," *Connecticut Libraries* 22 (Fall 1980): 2.

8. Mildred Frazier, "Yes, we charge fines," *Indiana Media Journal* 2 (Winter 1980): 18.

9. Janice Hankins, "Fines: a teaching tool," *Indiana Media Journal* 2 (Winter 1980): 17-18.

10. "Restoration of fines clicks at Sudbury," *Massachusetts Library Journal* 106 (October 1981): 1874-1875.

11. Frank Van Zanten, "Fine receipt is good PR," *Unabashed Librarian* 36 (1980): 3.

12. "Chicago Public gets tough with delinquent patrons," *Library Journal* 104 (December 1, 1979): 2504.

13. B. Steele, "Turning bad news into good news [amnesty days of Atlanta Public Library]," *Southeastern Librarian* 30 (Summer 1980): 94-95.

14. "DC fine-free week brings back 18,000," *Library Journal* 105 (October 15, 1980): 2146.

15. "18,000 overdue books returned to San Francisco Public Library," *Unabashed Librarian* 30 (1979): 26.

16. "St. Paul hits delinquents with service charges," *Library Journal* 106 (February 15, 1981): 404.

17. "Philadelphia using collection agency," *Wilson Library Bulletin* 56 (May 1982): 654-655.

18. "Mailgrams deliver long overdue books," *Unabashed Librarian* 35 (1980): 10. (Reprinted from Buffalo and Erie County Public Library *Bulletin*, February 1980.)

19. N. H. Petersen, "Upping the ante on overdues," *Library and Archival Security* 3 (Spring 1980): 25-27.

20. "Man jailed for library fines," *Unabashed Librarian* 30 (1979): 27.

21. "Chicago Public gets tough with delinquent patrons," *Library Journal* 104 (December 1, 1979): 2504.

22. "Conscience box," *Library Administrator's Digest*, volume 18, number 8 (no date): 62.

23. Will Manley, "Facing the Public," *Wilson Library Bulletin* (June 1983): 846-847.

24. "Mayor himself gets books back to Baltimore Library," *American Libraries* 13 (October 1982): 562-563.

25. W. D. Nelson, "Rooting for the home team brings returns [of overdue books]," *Wilson Library Bulletin* 57 (October 1982): 143.

26. Charlyne Van Ooosbree, "Book 'em! Case of the missing books," *Show Me Libraries* 31 (May 1980): 37-40.

27. Joy Guyatt, "Points and the implementation of an overdue policy," *Australian Academic and Research Libraries* 10 (September 1979): 179-184.

———Erratum. *Australian Academic and Research Libraries* 10 (December 1979): 224.

28. P. J. Hansel and R. Burgin, "Hard facts about overdues," *Library Journal* 108 (February 15, 1983): 349-352.

29. "Overdue study," *Unabashed Librarian* 33 (1979): 3.

Dealing with Defaulters

Art Goetz

ABSTRACT. The author discusses the use of small claims court for dealing with patrons who have overdue materials. Other solutions—multiple notices and billings, cablegrams, staff collectors—are dismissed as not cost-effective. The small claims court procedures for the state of Maryland are examined in detail, and the author's success through this method is documented. Similar successes in Maryland and North Carolina are cited.

I chose the term *defaulters* for the title of this article for more than one reason. First, I find the word intriguing, with an ''old English'' ring to it, and second, I think it most correctly identifies the culprits we'll be discussing at some length.[1] Finally, it is a rather quaint old phrase to be found in widespread use in library journals during Dewey's heyday.[2] It also does a much better job of identifying the problem at hand in one single word, surely far better than ''overdue offender'' or ''delinquent borrower,'' both of which have been overused in recent times. So defaulters they are and defaulters they shall remain—in this paper at least.

When I began researching this article in the tombs of the renowned Enoch Pratt Library in Baltimore last summer, I began with the thought that library defaulters surely must be an aged lot, and I felt confident in the thought that the problem of overdue materials must date back to the start of libraries and, more particularly for my research, that dealing sharply and positively with defaulters must also go back quite a long way.

And back it does go—to the first indexed journal record of the use of police in dealing with library defaulters in August 1887,[3] nearly

Art Goetz, Administrator, Wicomico County Free Library and Eastern Shore Regional Library, Salisbury, MD 21801.

one hundred years ago, when an article in *Library Journal* referred to the use of law enforcement two times a year in retrieving materials for the Bridgeport, Connecticut, library. The articles go on to state that Massachusetts and Rhode Island, in addition to Connecticut, had special ordinances and statutes with harsh fines from $1 to $25 or six months imprisonment for failing to return books to a library.

Even the British took note of our forceful methods in the old days. In an article in a London journal then called *Library Assistant*, the following remarks appear in a discussion about defaulters and collecting fines: "In the United States, after the lapse of a certain time, the police were requisitioned to make personal calls upon offenders."[4] The writer felt this unnecessary and suggested using messengers instead.

No matter the method used, it is evident from these findings that retrieving overdue materials is an ageless problem that will no doubt plague librarians until the truly electronic library is available for widespread use and we no longer check out hard copies to our patrons. At that time, other high tech problems will surface, problems which no doubt involve defaulting in some new ways.

For right now though we must consider facing the problem square on, as our worthy colleagues did back in Dewey's time, and issue court orders against the habitual defaulter. No other solution appears to be as cost-effective. Other methods of retrieval have included multiple notices and billings, cablegrams, threatening letters, staff collectors, sheriff and police collectors, phoned collection efforts or blitzes (with Baltimore's Mayor Schaefer included in one phoning session at the Enoch Pratt Library),[5] and using commercial collection agencies.

With the cost of postage continuing to escalate, multiple mailings should have long since fallen by the wayside. Cablegrams also seem costly, particularly if multiple use is made of them, as would probably be the case. Threatening letters may help but, to my thinking, must have some clout behind them, such as the court-issued subpoena, or they soon become ineffective as the public becomes aware that the threats are only idle messages.

Staff collectors, as well as police or sheriff intervention, are costly if paid by the library or with other public funds, and not many volunteers would stick to a distasteful job of harassing friends and neighbors. While the phone blitz technique is effective, it is expensive and time-consuming and necessitates multiple calls to reach most individuals, requiring an army of volunteers. In reality, commercial collection agencies only function as another step in a court-based approach. Their program is based on the use of "third party letters," under a service corporation's letterhead, to delinquent borrowers. The letter reminds the patron of his obligation either to return the materials or pay the replacement cost.

The third party involvement is supposed to have psychological impact since the letter will also mention the probable influence on credit ratings for those who fail to respond positively. The service is costly, with set fees for each letter and additional fees for follow-up as needed, including taking nonrespondents to court.[6] These fees are said to be recovered in retrieval success rates and patron payments. The point to remember here however is that you can do all this yourself. Why add a middleman's costs? The money paid by larger library systems for this type of service could be used more effectively by hiring a full-time collection employee to write the letters and initiate court proceedings. A library could also get other services out of such an employee as needed. (I shall say more about this later.)

This leaves us with the alternative of using the small claims court to retrieve nonreturned (stolen) materials. I use the term *stolen* advisedly, for I consider these defaulters as much thieves as those who actually steal rare and valuable manuscripts and monographs. Certainly the latter have enjoyed widespread notoriety in the profession of late. Witness the meeting in September 1983 at Oberlin College, attended by librarians, publishers, booksellers, the FBI, and INTERPOL for the expressed purpose of stopping book thefts.[7]

It was during this conference that mention was made of the epidemic proportions of such thefts today. One reason given for the rise in thefts was failure to prosecute. That very same reason is why we are in the fix we are in today with overdue materials—failure to prosecute!

It is our fault and our fault alone that patrons feel they have the right (yes, I said "right") to keep public property without concern or fear. Had we (and I certainly include myself) been doing our job properly all these hundred years or so and prosecuted whenever it was called for, the public would not be as complacent about this problem today. Of course, the reason we were not too concerned in the past was the lower cost of replacing books, as compared to the costs involved in court cases that may or may not produce results in the form of returned books or payments. But today's book prices make this form of retrieval far more appealing, particularly in severe or blatant default cases.

Over the years, others have seen the need to prosecute and would agree. Muriel Batchelder described the procedures for retrieving books through small claims court more than thirty years ago.[8] Joseph Eisner stated that "a subpoena from the court evokes a response unmatched by other methods," some twenty years ago.[9] C. Lamar Wallis, city library director in Memphis, Tennessee, complained of "the defiant attitude of some library patrons," only a bit more than ten years ago.[10] So a few have been trying to reeducate our patrons, and we ought to agree by starting a national campaign in all types of libraries to correct our own neglect in this regard.

How do we begin this war on defaulters and what is the best approach in the maze of legal tangles? I am not a lawyer, but I have devoted months to finding my way through the web of legal procedures, and will offer this trial-by-fire training to you for the price of reading on.

First of all, be prepared to spend two or three dozen hours in the beginning learning the legal ropes. I will tell you the shortcuts, but you must find your own way through your own District Court's particular method of entanglement.

Your first step is to visit your local State's Attorney and most particularly your Clerk of Court and his key staffers. Ask lots of questions, and if you can befriend the Clerk and his staff, you will have very little trouble and lots of help. Get to know them on a first name basis so you can call any time you have a question or need help with a form or procedure.

Discuss with them the type of small claims cases you have in mind and what you hope to accomplish. See the State's Attorney or one of his assistants to assure that you are proceeding legally and to ensure their help any time you have a case actually contested. (This has yet to happen to me in two years and about thirty-six cases.) The State's Attorney's office can also provide assistance in prosecuting your first case or two in court, although I feel that you will not need any outside help. You will be able to handle the case yourself, except perhaps if and when a patron contests with an attorney's help. Then you should have a lawyer to help present the case properly.

I have found only two logical ways to proceed that work well with defaulters: replevin action (which simply means "to recover property") or a tort action (to correct a wrong done to you). In the former action, you will be required to appear for a "show cause" hearing in which you explain to the judge why you are bringing this person to trial. The judge then decides whether you have good cause; whereupon you must return another day for the actual trial, if good cause was found, unless the defendant agrees to fully respond at the show cause hearing. The chance of a double appearance in replevin cases wastes your time and the court's time.

Therefore, the best method of action I have found, with the help of an attorney on our Library Board, is the tort action *with conversion cited*. This simply means that you claim that the defendant has held the library material overdue for so long, ignoring repeated notices in writing and by telephone (only if you have actually called), and has thereby converted the materials to his/her own property and that you are suing for all materials costs, court costs, special mailings, and phone call fees. You can even add staff hours spent on the problem if you wish and assign a dollar value to them. (If you use staff involvement fees, you had better document this so that you can properly respond if challenged. I don't include staff costs since I feel that we are public employees and that the retrieval of our public property is part of our duty as librarians.)

There is a general series of procedures involved in tort conversion cases that flows from the overdue notice and billings all the way through to supplementary hearings, attachment of wages or property, or to *fieri facias* (execution of a writ authorizing the sheriff to obtain satisfaction of a judgment by seizing and selling certain of the defendant's goods). These procedures are listed below in sequence. (The standard form numbers listed are Maryland standard form numbers. Your state's may vary.)

TORT PROCEDURES

1. Send your overdue notice or notices and billings, if you use bills.
2. If no response, send a normal mail letter notifying the patron of the value of the overdue items and fines due by giving a deadline to clear the account. Most patrons respond to this letter.
3. If some of the materials are returned, respond with a second letter thanking the patron and stating the outstanding fines owed and the cost of the books not returned.
4. If no response, send a warning letter showing the cost of the

overdue items. This letter should be sent certified with return receipt. (This method costs about $1.50.) These will get good response.

5. If no response, call and warn the patron that court proceedings will follow if the account is not cleared in a given number of days.

6. If no response, swear out the writ of tort. The cost is about $10, depending on claim value. Make this out in triplicate, keeping one copy for your file. A court hearing date will be assigned when you pay the fee.

7. The writ will cause the Sheriff's Department to issue a summons to the defendant in person. Generally, most people will respond before the court date, which is usually five to six weeks after the writ is sworn out.

8. If the patron responds, (1) retrieve all materials you can; (2) reduce the amount owed by the cost of the returned items; (3) make arrangements with the patron for payment in full or for an agreed-upon payment schedule (I suggest you devise an agreement form for the patron to sign); (4) after an agreement is set, call or write the Clerk of Court notifying him to continue the case, giving the name of defendant and case number; (5) follow up!—if payment is completed, notify the Clerk, and he will cancel the case; however, if the patron does not keep the payment schedule, you can reactivate the case by writing the Clerk stating that you wish the case re-opened (this should cost nothing, and the Sheriff's Department will issue another summons to trial, and you will receive a new court date by mail).

9. If the defendant does not appear for the original or follow-up trial, the court will issue a summary judgment against the defendant. You must then issue an order to record judgment and/or to file notice of lien (Form CV-75C), which costs $10 and causes notification to the defendant's employer to withhold the amounts needed to clear the debt. Garnishment must be completed within thirty days from the date of the writ. One caveat: in Maryland, you cannot legally attach wages of county or state employees, so the following step is required in such a case.

11. If the patron is a protected employee, you must swear out a petition for supplementary proceedings to begin monetary recovery. The cost of $10 includes a subpoena. This action brings you and the defendant together before a judge or his

appointee (usually the Clerk of Court). You are authorized to ask as many questions as you care to in order to determine the assets held by the defendant that can be attached in an amount sufficient to satisfy the judgment. If the defendant fails to appear for hearing, the court can issue a body attachment that requires a law officer to bring the defendant to court, or the court may ask you to issue a petition for contempt (at a cost of $5) that results in a subpoena again being served upon the defendant. I believe that if the defendant fails to appear on this order, the offense becomes a criminal offense and is dealt with accordingly. I have not yet gone past a contempt citation.

12. You must follow with a request to the court to record the judgment. There will probably be a $5 charge for this.

13. After the supplementary proceedings, attachments on judgment may be laid in the hands of anyone (banks included) until the judgment is satisfied. Each attachment costs $10. You may also ask the court to seize and sell certain goods which you believe the defendant owns. This is called *fieri facias* or execution. The cost is $10 to $20. You may also attach real estate, if you ask the court to file your judgment in the Circuit Court, as a lien (cost is $10).

Don't allow what may seem like a jumble of confusing procedures to frighten you away from attempting to prosecute defaulters. All of the costs involved are retrievable in costs assigned to the defendant in the issued warrants. Furthermore, something over 90 percent of the cases that have subpoenas issued never come to court trial; they are settled before the trial date. Once you get the hang of small claims retrieval, it is really not that difficult, and it does put clout in your retrieval process.

Best of all, the process I've explained has worked well for me. Beginning a crackdown with our board's blessing in July 1981, we went after thirty-one defaulters who held a total of 576 books and records. Only eleven of the cases required court proceedings (subpoenas issued). The others responded to letters or, in three cases, had moved and were not traceable. Of the overdues we went after, 467 were returned within the first year of the crackdown, a return rate of 81.1 percent. These returned materials had a value of nearly $5,000. In addition, we received payments of $1,014.85 in fines and fees.

Early in the crackdown, our efforts resulted in a jail sentence for one offender who had other charges against him. There was also a defaulter with fifty long overdue books. He returned all but one and paid fines and fees of more than $200.

We are now in our third year of the crackdown, and the retrieval rate remains at more than 80 percent, but the case load has diminished to only eight cases so far this year, with three of them actually carry-over cases from last year. By contrast, the first year we went after a total of thirty-one defaulters.

Others have reported similar successes. I wrote to all Maryland public library directors and several North Carolina directors to find out their experiences in prosecuting defaulters and to find out if they had taken such steps with offenders.

Judith C. Cooper, Public Services, Prince George's County Library, Maryland, wrote that they have referred offenders to the county's Office of Law when the outstanding materials value is at $150 or more, with considerable success since the mid-seventies. She further remarked that "The key to success with this sort of program is cooperation and communication between the library and the legal agencies." I couldn't agree more.

Durham County (North Carolina) library director Dale Gaddis wrote in her long response, "We began swearing out warrants because the number and value of failed to return books was so high that not doing anything more about it than we were doing seemed to me to represent irresponsibility on my part as library director." She went on to say that though she does not like swearing out warrants, she feels it necessary in some cases and therefore will continue this procedure. I admire that kind of determination and dedication in doing a somewhat distasteful but certainly necessary task.

Kenneth Reading, director of the Public Library of Johnston County and Smithfield (North Carolina) reported a reduction of 20 percent in overdues since 1981 by using letters from the Sheriff with delinquent accounts. He further stated his people "resorted to this action to reduce the escalating overdues problem and have had no adverse public reaction." I have also found the latter to be true; we estimate that our crackdown has reduced the overdues problem by 20 to 25 percent.

Mary L. Barnett, director of the Burke County Public Library (North Carolina), writes that she has experienced "adverse criticism or reaction by the public. Most people simply cannot believe either that a person would take library books, or that we would be so petty as to take them to court." But she does not let this deter her since she correctly feels "the whole problem is enormous" and that we must do something.

Finally, in a somewhat negative reply, Carolyn M. Wiker, director of a neighboring county library in Chestertown, Maryland, writes that her success rate was poor in her prior library in Adams County (Pennsylvania) because many of the people moved or had no assets. However, I would not let factors like that deter you from trying. It is only through the widespread use of prosecution that we can ever hope to change the complacent attitude of the library public. Why should they be concerned and act responsibly if librarians do not show concern and act responsibly?

I appreciate the candid responses of these librarians. But the total of ten responses (half were not useful) out of my thirty-three requests for information indicates that far too few concerned librarians are involved in this kind of effort. It is our responsibility as librarians to force this issue, and those who are "letting George do all the work" are contributing to the defaulter problem while being irresponsible custodians of their public trust. As one librarian put it in an article in *Unabashed Librarian*: "Librarians must either take drastic measures or kiss off the overdue books."[11]

REFERENCES

1. The OED defines a defaulter as "one who is guilty of default; esp. one who fails to perform some duty or obligation legally required of him." *Oxford English Dictionary*, S.V. "defaulter."

2. W. K. Stetson, "Delinquent Borrowers," *Library Journal* 14 (1889): 403-4; or Vale, G. F. "On the track of the defaulter," *Library Assistant* 5 (1907): 251-2.

3. Ibid.

4. R. Dumenil, "Defaulters," *Library Assistant* 12 (1915): 12.

5. "Mayor himself gets books back to Baltimore library," *American Libraries* 13 (October 1982): 562-3.

6. For method and approximate costs, see "Philadelphia using collection agency," *Wilson Library Bulletin* 56 (May 1982): 654-5; or "Retrieving overdues through a collection agency: one academic library's approach," *Library Journal* 108 (November 1, 1983): 2030-1.

7. See *LJ Library Hotline* 12 (October 24, 1983): 1; and "Librarians meet to fight book thieves," *American Libraries* 16 (November 1983): 648.

8. Muriel G. Batchelder, "Retrieving books through small claims court," *Library Journal* 77 (February 1, 1952): 181-2.

9. Joseph Eisner, "Recovery by court action," *Wilson Library Bulletin* 37 (February 1963): 485-6.

10. "Delinquent library patrons face stiff fines & jail," *Library Journal* 97 (May 1, 1972): 1661.

11. Charlyne Van Oosbree, "Book 'Em! Or case of the missing books," *Unabashed Librarian* #40 (1981): 15-6.

Baltimore County Public Library and the Delinquent Borrower

Marilyn Murray

ABSTRACT. This article explains how the Baltimore County (Maryland) Public Library has employed small claims court measures in its overdues procedures. The library attempts to contact patrons with $40 or more in overdue materials. If the patron cannot be contacted and if the patron does not respond to letters, court action is initiated. The results of this approach are documented, and forms are appended.

Retrieval of overdue materials is a part of every public library's responsibility to the taxpayer. Procedures vary widely for meeting the obligation.

In the Baltimore County (Maryland) Public Library, the rate of overdues has remained relatively stable as a proportion of the total circulation. The circulation, however, has steadily increased to 9,000,000 (fiscal year 1983), resulting in an increasing number of overdue items.

Before writing off losses as a recurring expense of circulation services, Baltimore County added a further step in its normal overdue collection procedures. Small claims court action was begun in February 1983 for a very selective number of serious offenders.

The Circulation Control Department, which handles all of the overdue notices and collection procedures, was given permission to seek litigation only as a last resort after all of the usual attempts to retrieve materials have failed. Prescribed steps are followed before any court action is taken.

A notification enclosed with the overdue notice mailed to the patron warns that court action may be taken for failure to return or pay for library materials. (See Figure 1.) If no response is forth-

Marilyn Murray, Publications and Promotion Department, Baltimore County Public Library, Towson, MD 21204.

51

FIGURE 1

BALTIMORE COUNTY PUBLIC LIBRARY

This is your only notification. Until the problem/s listed on the enclosed notice has been cleared, your borrowing privileges have been temporarily suspended.

Only a fine will be charged for overdue items returned in usable condition. For each item which is lost, you will be charged the replacement cost shown on your notice, plus a 50¢ service fee.

If you have any questions, please refer to the branch identified on the enclosed notice.

Failure to respond to this notice within 7 days may result in referral to BCPL's Collector for Overdue Materials who may begin court action for return of or payment for library materials.

12/83

---

coming for delinquent accounts of $40 and up in replacement cost of materials, the Circulation Control Department tries to contact the patron by phone to request return of the materials. Following this, the collector visits the patron's residence. If no one is at home, the collector leaves a flyer informing the patron of his visit and warning that failure to return the materials within seven days will result in court action. (See Figure 2.)

If none of these attempts is completely successful, a form letter is sent to the patron whether or not telephone contact has been made. (See Appendix 1.) The borrower is given seven days from the date of the letter to respond, after which court action is initiated. Where a patron responds to the letter with a partial return of materials or returns with no fines paid, a follow-up letter is sent to advise the patron of the current status of delinquence. (See Appendix 2.)

If no response is made, Baltimore County Public Library submits to the County's Office of Law a complete history of the patron's borrowing record including a list of the materials, length of time they have been out, cost of replacement, and documentation of the number of times and the dates attempts have been made to contact the patron about his/her overdue materials. (See Figure 3.) A county attorney signs the petition, and copies are sent to the court and to the patron; the library retains a copy.

The library then requests the sheriff to serve a summons on the delinquent borrower. Since it must be served directly to the borrower, a sheriff's deputy is often unable to do so even after a couple of attempts. A certified letter, notifying the person of the court action, is then sent. (See Appendix 3.) If the certified letter is undeliverable, the library's collector, who is deputized to do so, can serve the summons. If and when he cannot reach the person after several tries, he can get the court's permission to serve the summons to anyone over 18 years of age in the house.

Defendants have four choices: (1) clear their records prior to the hearing date, in which case the library withdraws its petition; (2) partially clear their records, in which case the library reserves the right to continue with legal action; (3) notify the court that they will

FIGURE 2

BALTIMORE COUNTY PUBLIC LIBRARY

A staff member visited your home today as a follow-up regarding long overdue library materials. These materials were charged out on the card of: _____
from the _____ Branch.

Our primary concern is the return of this material as soon as possible so that other library users may benefit from it.

Arrangements can be made, if necessary, for the payment of fines at a later date. Materials can be returned to any branch of the Baltimore County Public Library, or if you desire, we can pick up the material at your home.

Failure to respond to this notice within 7 days will lead to court action for the return of the materials or their cost, plus court costs.

Please call Mr. Warren Edwards at the Library's Administrative Offices, 296-8500, to discuss this matter.

We appreciate your cooperation.

3/83

FIGURE 3

ZEBRA #:_____

NAME:_____

STREET: _____

CITY, STATE,

ZIP CODE: _____

TELEPHONE #: _____

DUE DATE(S):_____

AND TYPE OF

MATERIAL:_____

COST OF

MATERIAL:_____

OWNING

AGENCY(IES):_____

BILLS SENT: _____

COLLECTOR

RECEIVED:_____

COLLECTOR

LEFT NOTICE: _____

PHONE CALL

TO PATRON: _____

REPLY:_____

PHONE CALL

TO PATRON: _____

REPLY:_____

DATE:

appear in their defense at the hearing, in which case the library will have staff representation at the hearing; (4) make no response.

If a defendant takes no action and does not appear at the hearing, a summary judgment for the library is issued by the court, and no staff member needs to attend. To date, 12 cases have been presented in court, and in each, judgment was rendered in favor of the library.

When judgment is found against the borrower, the library files the judgment to appear on the person's credit rating after a 30-day waiting period. To date, the library has not moved to collect through garnishment of wages and the like, but this could be a further action.

The result of the small claims court threat and information on successful prosecution has been an increased return of materials formerly written off as losses. Thirty-eight percent of the recipients of

1,500 letters threatening court action have returned their overdue materials with a total value of $34,000. Only 15 percent of the letters have been undeliverable because the addressee had moved without forwarding address or the address was invalid.

The Circulation Control Department worked closely with the County's Office of Law to set up the guidelines for the procedures, establish the forms for paperwork records, and in general determine the library's and the Office of Law's roles in their joint participation in court action.

The procedures are time-consuming, especially to verify the accuracy of the library's claim from initiation of action to hearing date. With 23 branches reporting delinquencies and delinquent borrower interaction with the library possible at any outlet, collection of information on individual cases by Circulation Control Department is a labor-intensive job. The library has chosen to concentrate on relatively few court cases to sustain its 100 percent rate of successful prosecutions. As public awareness of this procedure grows, the success rate in prosecutions should have a positive effect on the return of overdue materials by persons subject to court action.

*APPENDIX 1**

You have a record of overdue materials from the Baltimore County Public Library. We have been unable to contact you by telephone regarding this matter. You are responsible for   items valued at   that were checked out from the

Failure to respond to this notice (i.e., prompt return of the materials or payment of the replacement cost) within 7 days will lead to court action. Arrangements can be made, if necessary, for the payment of fines at a later date.

If you need clarification of your delinquency record, call the Circulation Control Office (296-8500, Ext. 278), Monday-Saturday, 9:00 a.m.-5:30 p.m.

Sincerely,

Kimberly A. Evans
Head, Circulation Control

KAE/sf

---

*All form letters in Appendixes 1-3 were sent on Baltimore County Public Library Stationery.

APPENDIX 2

We have received a partial return of material which you had long overdue from the collection of the Baltimore County Public Library.

Since other material you have is still overdue, your record is not totally cleared, and you will be refused borrowing privileges in this library system. Your record can be cleared by the return of the remaining outstanding material or the payment of the replacement costs.

Any fines, as well as any replacement costs, which are owed may be paid using our Partial Payment Plan. An initial minimum payment of $5.00 must be made, and 20% of the original total must be paid at each use of your library card. At the time of each payment, you may check out 2 pieces of material. All charges must be paid within six months. Please ask for the clerical supervisor at your branch to make arrangements if you wish to use this plan.

We reserve the right to continue legal action to recover Baltimore County Public Library property.

Yours truly,

Kimberly A. Evans
Head, Circulation Control

KAE/sf

APPENDIX 3

You have a record of long overdue materials from the Baltimore County Public Library. A summary is attached.

Unless you return these materials, or pay for their replacement costs, by   we will initiate court action on   on the basis of your unauthorized retention of county property.

If you need clarification of your delinquency record, call the Circulation Control Office (296-8500, Ext. 278), Monday through Friday, 8:30 a.m.-5:00 p.m.

Cordially yours,

Charles W. Robinson
Director

CWR/sf

Three Libraries
and Overdues Law

Patsy Hansel

ABSTRACT. The author examines three North Carolina public libraries—Cumberland County, Dare County, and Catawba County—and their experiences with the legal side of overdues. Cumberland County's procedure of taking delinquent patrons to court is outlined, and a particular case is examined. Dare County's local County Attorney had a special law enacted for that county by the 1983 General Assembly; the implications for the library's procedures are noted. Attention is given to the enacting by Catawba County's Commissioners of a local ordinance governing overdue library materials.

(*Editor's note*: This article was compiled with information provided by Ricki Brown, Head of Adult Services, Cumberland County Public Library, Fayetteville, NC; Amy Frazer, Dare County Librarian, Manteo, NC; and John Pritchard, Director, Catawba County Public Library, Newton, NC.)

Overdues are a problem in any library. Cumberland County Public Library is no exception. The results of the Hansel-Burgin survey of 1981 showed that Cumberland had the lowest return rate among libraries studied. This factor plus a high level of staff frustration forced the library to carefully examine overdue procedures. After consulting the County Attorney, the library staff adopted the following procedures:

1. Postcards are mailed to patrons when materials fall two weeks past due. The materials are listed by title on the postcard. (See Appendix 1.)
2. Statements are mailed to patrons when the materials fall four weeks past due. The statement lists the materials, the cost(s) of the materials, the date the materials were due, and gives a date

---

Patsy Hansel, Assistant Director, Cumberland County Public Library, Fayetteville, NC 28302.

57

(two weeks from the date of the statement) when the matter
will be forwarded to the County Attorney's office. (See Appendix 2.)

3. When materials are six weeks past due, a copy of the statement is forwarded to the County Attorney's office. The County Attorney writes each offending patron asking for the return
of the materials and stating the consequences of the failure to
do so. (See Appendix 3.)

The aforementioned procedures increased Cumberland's return
rate by 10 percent the first year. Collection of fines increased approximately 28 percent.

Cumberland's staff were pleased with the increase in the rate of
book return, but they were also concerned about the remaining
patrons who continued to abuse their privileges and ignore the
library's notices. As the signer of each final notice, the County Attorney also said that he was concerned that "some library patrons
are building up private library collections at County expense." It
was at his initiative and with his guidance that library staff began to
prepare for prosecution.

Staff gathered copies of library registrations, book cards, and
statements. Shelves were checked and rechecked for the missing
items. It was decided to prosecute patrons with a minimum of $50
worth of outstanding materials. The County Attorney wrote one
more letter to twenty patrons advising them to return the materials
within the next three weeks to avoid prosecution. At the end of the
three-week period, ten individuals had responded, and summonses
were issued for the remainder. Court dates were set, and library
staff anxiously awaited the unknown.

On Cumberland's first day in court, two cases were to be heard.
The judge did ask for information such as the dates notices were
sent, when the materials were due, the cost of the materials. The
careful and detailed records kept by the staff were invaluable. In the
first case, the patron had returned the materials after receiving the
summons. The judge fined the individual $50 plus court costs.

In the second case, the defendant did not show up, and the case
was continued. Library staff later learned that this patron had hired
a lawyer and intended to plead innocent on the grounds that she had
checked out the items for a niece and that the niece had failed to
return them. The patron also maintained that she had not received
any of the notices the library had sent. The staff learned the patron's

story from letters that various members of her family wrote in her defense to the local papers. Except for these letters, the library's legal action received very positive publicity locally.

The second time this patron's case came up, she once again failed to appear. Outside in the corridor, the County Attorney told the library staff that she had one more chance to appear, and that if she didn't, he would have her bound over to Superior Court on a felony charge. This sort of statement along with others from the County Attorney such as, " 'If they can't pay the fine, they shouldn't do the crime' is our motto at the Cumberland County Public Library," caused some soul-searching among the librarians involved. The librarians just wanted the books back; none of them *wanted* to be spending their days in court behind lawyers calling their heretofore patrons liars and cheats. Once initiated, however, the legal process moved inexorably. The librarians hoped it was toward a conclusion they could support.

On her third chance, the patron with the lawyer did appear in court. After testimony by the library staff, followed by that of the patron and several members of her extended family, the judge decided to find no probable cause to pursue the case against the patron, but referred the matter of the niece's culpability to juvenile court. Although the books had been returned and the fines paid, the library received an additional $85 restitution through the juvenile court.

The publicity surrounding the court cases has definitely resulted in a higher return of books. The day after the news of the court cases hit the media, the library system had its highest one-day take of fines ever. During the second round of overdues letters since prosecution of these cases began, only one patron still has over $50 worth of items outstanding and is eligible to receive a summons. In the first round, ten summonses were initiated.

Unfortunately, not all the summonses were served, as some individuals had moved. However, if such a person is ever stopped for a traffic violation or something similar, the outstanding summons will surface and be served.

In another North Carolina library, Dare County, the local County Attorney did not feel comfortable prosecuting under the North Carolina law (see Appendix 4), and had a special law for his county enacted in the 1983 session of the General Assembly. (See Appendix 5.)

A copy of the law, sent by certified mail, appears on the library's third notice sent six weeks after material is due. The patron has thirty days after that to clear his record. The cost of the certified letter is passed on to the patron.

Since the library began using this law in October 1983, Dare County's overdues have dropped significantly—3 to 4 books a month are still overdue out of a circulation of 5-6,000 a month. So far, only one patron has not returned the material within 30 days, but that person has moved away, and the County Attorney is trying to decide if the matter is worth pursuing. The drawback to the procedure is the rigid schedule and strict attention to detail that must be maintained.

Another option for skittish library attorneys is an ordinance enacted by a local government body. After consulting the North Carolina Department of Justice, the Catawba County Public Library decided to have their Board of County Commissioners enact such an ordinance. (See Appendix 6.)

Catawba prints an excerpt from the ordinance on their second and final notice. They have followed through with a warrant in only one case. That case involved a film that a patron insisted he had returned but which the library had not received. After the patron spent a brief stint in the local jail, the film appeared on the library's porch. The library was informed that they could not drop charges at that point but that their failure to appear in court to pursue the charges would have the same result. They chose not to appear.

APPENDIX 1

NOTICE

Please return the following overdue book(s) drawn on your library card:

CUMBERLAND COUNTY PUBLIC LIBRARY
FAYETTEVILLE, NORTH CAROLINA 28302

You will be billed for any books not returned. When library is closed, please use book return.

APPENDIX 2

April 24, 1984

You checked out and have not returned library materials shown on the attached notice. Unlawfully detaining public library materials is a crime punishable as a misdemeanor or a felony pursuant to North Carolina General Statute 14-398.

Please make all returns or payments directly to Ms. Ricki Brown at the Anderson Street Branch Library, Fayetteville, North Carolina. If you have not done so by May 4, 1984, the appropriate criminal proceedings will be *immediately* initiated against you.

Yours truly,

GARRIS NEIL YARBOROUGH
County Attorney

GNY/ejb
Attachment
cc: Major Charles Smith, Detective Bureau
    Cumberland County Sheriff's Department

APPENDIX 3

NOTICE OF PUBLIC LIBRARY MATERIALS NOT RETURNED
(Please return the top portion of this statement with your remittance.)

Library Materials	Price
641.66--Variety Meats	$11.95
641.5---Japanese garnishes	12.95
641.8---Terrines, Pates, and Galantines	11.95
641.66--Wheat & poultry entrees for food service menu planning	14.95
Processing Fee ($3.00 per accessioned title)	12.00
TOTAL	$63.80

The materials listed above were borrowed by you from the Public Library and have not been returned. The materials were due 3-1-84. If you return the aforementioned materials in good condition you will only be charged an overdue fine of $1.50 per item, otherwise you must pay the amount shown above.

In registering to borrow Public Library materials, you became responsible for the return of all borrowed materials at the end of the loan period or if lost or damaged to pay for them. Unlawfully detaining library materials is a crime, punishable as a misdemeanor or a felony pursuant to North Carolina General Statutes 14-398. Failure to respond to this notice by 4-12-84 will result in the notice being referred to the County Attorney's Office for the appropriate legal action.

cc: County Attorney

APPENDIX 4

§14-398. Theft or destruction of property of public libraries museums, etc.

Any person who shall steal or unlawfully take or detain, or willfully or maliciously or wantonly write upon, cut, tear, deface, disfigure, soil, obliterate, break or destroy, or who shall sell or buy or receive, knowing the same to have been stolen, any book, document, newspaper, periodical, map, chart, picture, portrait, engraving, statue, coin, medal, apparatus, specimen, or other work of literature or object of art or curiosity deposited in a public library, gallery, museum, collection, fair or exhibition, or in any department of office of State or local government, or in a library, gallery, museum, collection, or exhibition, belonging to any incorporated college or university, or any incorporated institution devoted to educational, scientific, literary, artistic, historical or charitable purposes, shall, if the value of the property stolen, detained, sold, bought or received knowing same to have been stolen, or if the damage done by writing upon, cutting, tearing, defacing, disfiguring, soiling, obliterating, breaking or destroying any such property, shall not exceed fifty dollars ($50.00), be guilty of a misdemeanor and upon conviction shall be fined or imprisoned in the discretion of the court. If the value of the property stolen, detained, sold or received knowing same to have been stolen, or the amount of damage done in any of the ways or manners herinabove set out, shall exceed the sum of fifty dollars ($50.00), the person committing same shall be punished as a Class H felon. (1935, c. 300; 1943, c. 543; 1979, c. 760, s. 5.)

[North Carolina General Statutes]

APPENDIX 5

1981 SESSION OF THE GENERAL ASSEMBLY OF NORTH CAROLINA

AN ACT REGARDING RETENTION AND DESTRUCTION OF LIBRARY BOOKS IN DARE COUNTY.

"A person is guilty of a misdemeanor punishable by a fine of not more than fifty dollars ($50.00), public service working in the library at the direction of the librarian for not more than 24 hours as a condition of probation, imprisonment for not more than 30 days, or any combination thereof if he:

1. Willfully or intentionally fails to return to a public library any library item within 30 days after the librarian or his agent has served by certified mail or delivered in person a written notice that the time for which that library item may be kept has expired: or
2. willfully or intentionally removes from the premises of a public library any library item without checking it out in accordance with the posted regulations of the library: or
3. willfully or wantonly damages, defaces, mutilates, or otherwise destroys any library item.

A copy of this statute shall be posted in all public libraries and shall appear on the face of all notices mailed or delivered pursuant to subdivision (1).

For purposes of this subsection, library item, includes any book, picture, engraving, map, magazine, pamphlet, newspaper, manuscript, or object of art or of historical significance, or any audiovisual or other equipment owned or in use by the library.

This subsection applies to Dare County only."

This act shall become effective October 1, 1983.

APPENDIX 6

ORDINANCE

RETENTION, REMOVAL, DESTRUCTION, ETC.,
OF LIBRARY MATERIALS A
MISDEMEANOR

BE IT ORDAINED BY THE COUNTY COMMISSIONERS OF
CATAWBA COUNTY:

A. (1) Whoever receives or becomes responsible for any library materials belonging to any public library in Catawba County or any library or branch thereof supported wholly or in part by the public funds of Catawba County, and who willfully fails to return any such library materials to the library or branch thereof from which it was received for a period of fifteen (15) days after mailing or delivering in person a notice in writing from the librarian or assistant librarian of such library or branch thereof that the time for which such library materials may be kept under library regulations has expired, or

(2) Whoever willfully or intentionally removes from the premises of such library or branch thereof any library materials without charging them out in accordance with the regulations of such library or branch thereof, or

(3) Whoever willfully or wantonly damages, defaces, mutilates, or otherwise destroys any library materials, whether on the library premises or on loan, shall be guilty of a misdemeanor and upon conviction, shall be punished by a fine of not more than fifty dollars ($50.00) or imprisonment for not more than thirty (30) days provided, that the notice required by this Ordinance shall bear upon its face a copy of this Ordinance.

B. For the purpose of this Ordinance, the term "library materials" shall be defined to include, without limitation, any book, plate, picture, engraving, map, magazine, pamphlet, newspaper, manuscript, film, recording, specimen, work of literature, object d'art, item of historical significance, item of curiosity, slide, projector, opaque projector, overhead projector, movie projector, film-strips, slides, recorders, sound equipment, transparencies, micro-forms, audio-visual equipment, art materials, supplies, equipment of any sort, or any other item owned by or loaned to such library or branch thereof.

C. In all indictments for violations of the provisions of this Ordinance, it shall not be necessary to allege or prove that the item not returned was lawfully received by such person from any such public library, but only that the person came into possession of the same, knowing that the same belonged to such public library, and the failure of any person to return any such item after written demand as set forth above shall be prima facie proof that the person possessing said item acted willfully in failing to return such item within said fifteen (15) days period.

Overdues and Academic Libraries:
Matters of Access
and Collection Control

Jean Walter Farrington

ABSTRACT. How overdues are dealt with in an academic library often depends on which group of borrowers is involved. For student borrowers, reducing overdues requires an appropriate loan period (including study carrels for graduate students) and certain punitive measures, such as fines, revoking borrowing privileges, or blocking students from registering. Faculty and staff overdues are more difficult to resolve, and individual cases may be very time-consuming. Outside borrowers can be dealt with in traditional ways (fines, revoked privileges), but serious problems can develop.

It might well be said that overdue books are the bane of the circulation librarian's existence. The librarian wants the books accounted for, the patron wants a particular book that another patron has, and no one is happy. Overdue books are undoubtedly one of the biggest circulation problems for academic libraries. How they are handled often depends on which group of borrowers is involved. Before dealing with several distinct groups of academic library users, let us consider several facets of the overdue problem as it relates to academic libraries in general.

1. *Overdue books are a serious problem only when another patron is denied access to a particular title.*

Although circulation librarians spend a great deal of time worrying about the number of overdue books and working to get them returned, most overdue books are a collection control problem rather than an access problem. When a book that a given patron has on loan is needed by another patron and is *not* returned on time, then it

---

Jean Walter Farrington, Head, Serials Department, University of Pennsylvania, Philadelphia, PA 19104 (formerly, Acting Head of Circulation).

becomes a case of unavailability of material. Academic libraries exist to serve the scholarly and research needs of their clientele, and access to material is the most important service they provide. The overdue book that someone else wants has crossed the dividing line from being a collection control or inventory problem to becoming a service question.

2. *Academic libraries satisfy the needs of their patrons by means of a great diversity of titles.*

In a public library, there are usually more patrons wanting the same small core of titles than is the case in an academic library. Since academic libraries serve a community of researchers and students, the collection needs are more varied and disparate. A given title in an academic library may be checked out once this year and then not again for ten years. Further, it is not uncommon for a graduate student to borrow twenty to thirty books for dissertation research and then be able to renew them continually for two to three years without anyone else ever recalling them. Some or all of the books may become overdue at some point during that two to three year period, but unless another individual wants a particular one, their overdue status is not a cause for alarm, at least not if one's emphasis is on access to material rather than on inventory control. (One does hope, of course, that all the books are returned when the dissertation is handed in.)

Even in an academic library, however, there are some groups of users who require access to the same materials. Special arrangements (such as reserve book collections, non-circulating seminar collections, or assigned study carrels for in-house loans) are usually made to handle these situations. Overdue policies for these special arrangements are sometimes more stringent, as in the case of reserve books, or non-existent, as in the case of carrel books.

3. *Academic libraries (and other types, too) operate on the basic principle of cooperation.*

The privilege of borrowing books from an academic library is just that, a privilege extended to students, faculty, and staff. For the immediate university community, no separate fee is levied for taking materials away from the library. The library sets a specified loan period as a way to impose order and structure on the system and simultaneously request cooperation from the patron. A patron may then keep material for a stated length of time provided he or she plays by the rules. The rules state that if the individual patron tells the library ahead of time that he/she would like to keep a book longer, the extension is usually agreed to, unless someone else has requested it. This system depends on users feeling obligated to return books on time either because they wish to avoid penalties (such as fines) or because they feel some sense of community responsibility.

There is no doubt that dealing with overdues is troublesome and time-consuming. Different approaches often work better with different types of users. In order to focus more on how overdues in academic libraries are handled, three separate groups of users will be considered: (1) students, both undergraduates and graduates; (2) faculty and administrators; and (3) unaffiliated or outside borrowers.

STUDENT BORROWERS

Students are a transient population within the academic institution, but in most academic libraries, they account for the largest percentage of books borrowed. Within the student group, graduate students borrow significantly more books than undergraduates. As one might expect, borrowing by graduate students is more narrowly focused on their immediate subject area, while undergraduates borrow more widely across the collection. Dealing with student overdues requires a combination of humor, tact, and flexibility within the framework of reasonable loan and overdue policies. Reducing the total number of overdues may require carefully setting or juggling the length of the loan period over time in combination with appropriate punitive measures.

Given the different use of the collection, many academic libraries opt for longer loan periods for graduate students. For example, the undergraduate loan period may be three or four weeks and the graduate loan eight weeks or a full semester. The intent of this should be to allow the student adequate time to read and use the book without misplacing it for forgetting its whereabouts. Since graduate students borrow more books, allowing them a longer loan period also reduces the number of renewals the circulation staff has to process.

For graduate students who need masses of material, the study carrel may be another answer to the overdue problem. At the University of Pennsylvania, graduate students may apply for an open study desk with one shelf and may charge books to that location. It is understood that the books are not to be taken out of the library. The

books are all due 12/31/99 and hence do not become overdue unless
recalled by another patron. In the meantime, the books are always
available in the library for anyone to use. If a recall for another
patron is ignored, the library staff will eventually remove the book
for the second patron. In this way, access to the material is provided
at all times while doing away with overdues.

For both undergraduates and graduate students, there is the matter of fines and other penalties used as incentives or disciplinary
measures to get books back. While these penalties have some effect,
there are also drawbacks. Many libraries that do impose fines also
allow a grace period of a day or two before the fines actually are
charged. This is desirable but may, in effect, mean that everyone
automatically adds the length of the grace period onto the original
loan. When the loan period for students has been determined, there
is then the matter of how many notices of what types (overdue, bill,
fine) will be sent when.

In dealing with overdues, it is important that the library establish
a reasonable cycle of notices. For example, first overdues are sent
out when the book is one week overdue; second overdues are sent at
three weeks overdue and warn about possible replacement charges;
third overdues or bills are sent at six or eight weeks and list replacement costs; and a final notice is a referral to some office or agency
outside the library. With an on-line circulation system, it is easy for
a library to set up and monitor this type of notice cycle. One can
study the statistics on the number of notices printed and determine
what the ratios are. For example, at the University of Pennsylvania,
normally about three times as many first notices are printed in a
given year as second notices. When the bill notice is printed, there
are about one-third to one-half as many as the total number of second notices. This ratio of first notices to second notices to third has
held relatively constant for the past several years.

Without some prior experience or statistics, it is difficult to determine the precise point in time when the first notice should be
sent. It is a question of waiting long enough, but not too long, to get
maximum return. Another reason for having stated loan periods,
alluded to previously, beyond the question of access, is the need for
collection control. Most academic libraries of any size cannot afford
to do regular inventories of all or even part of their stacks; the over-
due/notice process alerts the library to what is missing and needs to
be replaced.

In addition to fines, most libraries also assess a cost for replacing a given book after some long time overdue (six to eight weeks, for example). This can be an incentive to get the book back since paying a fine would be cheaper than paying the replacement cost. There are, however, some users who believe that paying the replacement cost (almost always less than the actual cost of the book) is an inexpensive way to build up one's personal library. One could make a weak argument that books should never be overdue unless recalled by another patron. By not doing this, however, libraries show their concern for the other aspect of overdue materials, control of the collection. Librarians feel, and justifiably so, that it is important to know where a given book is at any time and are distrustful of patrons who do not frequently reaffirm their possession of the material. Therefore, most libraries have instituted renewal procedures.

How *do* academic libraries cope with students and excessive numbers of overdue books? For some students, just knowing that a book is overdue and is going to cost money is not enough by itself to make them return all items on time. The timely reminders contained in the various notices have some effect, but other incentives are required. The most obvious incentive, and the one most easily effected, is the suspension of borrowing privileges. In this day of on-line systems, suspending borrowing privileges can be done automatically by the computer when the student reaches a certain number of overdue books or a certain number of books at the bill stage. This can be effective, but there are ways around it too, for example, the ploy of having a friend check out any other books needed. Sometimes, however, the student has all the books he needs and has no desire to borrow anything else that semester. For the library, the "bottom line" is having the books back, and this situation of lacking critical titles can become frustrating for all concerned. There are usually two courts of last resort on the campus: the registrar and the bursar. The registrar is certainly the most effective referral since being prevented from registering for the next semester or being unable to request a transcript really cramps a student's style. Failing the registrar, sending replacement charges for overdue books to the bursar to be added to the student's term bill usually generates a positive response unless a parent pays the whole bill without question. Even with this last option, the student may still return all the books and pay a substantially reduced fine instead of replacement costs.

While the delinquent student borrower is a problem, the library nonetheless has these clear-cut options: revoke borrowing priv-

ileges; refer charges to the university accounts office; or block
students from registering. The case against faculty and staff is less
easily resolved.

FACULTY AND ADMINISTRATIVE STAFF

The rules for faculty and administrative staff are often less well-
defined than those for students; faculty and administrators often
have higher expectations of the library's service and treatment of
them given their position in the community. Consequently, most
academic libraries treat their faculty and staff with some deference
and accord them privileges beyond the norm. The faculty/staff, in
turn, to some extent view themselves as the true scholars on the
campus and as such reserve to themselves the undisputed right of
unlimited access to the collection. This is perhaps a slight overstate-
ment, but academic libraries generally recognize this specialness
with an extended loan period, unlimited renewals, and often no fines
for overdue books.

The usual approach to faculty/staff borrowing is to define a loan
period of a semester or a year and then allow these individuals to
renew their books indefinitely. This indefinite renewal is accomplished by having the faculty/staff bring in their books or by allowing them to annotate a list of what they have out with those items
they wish to retain. Faculty/staff, like any other group of borrowers, are expected to respond to recalls from other patrons wish-
ing to use material that they have. Since the percentage of borrowing by faculty and administrators is fairly small, the numbers of
overdues for which they are accountable is not as great as with the
student population. On the other hand, most academic libraries are
reluctant to use punitive measures against faculty/staff. There are
usually no fines, no referrals to other university offices, and only
occasionally a complete suspension of borrowing privileges. The
main exception to this less than stringent policy generally comes
with overdue recalled library books; many libraries are tightening
up on all borrowers who fail to return books needed by other
patrons.

Even though the number of overdues is smaller, individual faculty cases can sometimes be very difficult and time-consuming. Time
and tact are expended in dealing with a few troublesome individuals.
With faculty overdues, there also seems to be a greater likelihood
that the items will be lost or incorporated with the borrower's own
books. Personal phone calls, pleas for cooperation and the like, with

a call to the department chairperson as a last resort, are tried and sometimes successful methods at many libraries. Like the student overdues, ordinary faculty overdues are not a problem provided the books are still in the professor's office and not lost or loaned to a student in Iowa. Unfortunately, some few faculty are less than cooperative, and if a book has been recalled by another faculty member, they are unwilling to let that person have the book and risk his/her keeping it out forever. Administrative staff generally have the same privileges as faculty, but probably do less borrowing overall and do not cause as much difficulty. One might risk saying that they are better team players, given the nature of their positions, and less apt to be testy. Dealing with faculty and staff also has a public relations aspect that can contribute to an uncomfortable tension for the librarian. It is probably necessary to recognize this but not let it paralyze one's actions.

Interestingly enough, a recent study done at Indiana University confirmed something most circulation librarians already knew about faculty borrowing. The study found that "graduate students recalled almost 3.5 times more books than faculty and that 41 percent of all books recalled were charged out to faculty."[1] This would not be unusual if faculty accounted for 40 percent of the borrowing activity. During the four months of the project, however, "faculty charged out. . .8 percent of all books charged out."[2] This study tends to justify the feeling circulation librarians have that some faculty are very uncooperative borrowers. Trying to appeal to them through their peers, through actions of the library faculty advisory committee or through letters or phone calls are not as successful as one would like. This is combined with the fact that librarians do not send their faculty borrowers to the equivalent of the bursar or the registrar. If a faculty member leaves the institution with books in tow, only then may he or she be referred to a collection agency.

UNAFFILIATED BORROWERS

In some ways, the most interesting group of borrowers are the unaffiliated or outside borrowers. They are interesting partly for their diversity. Many, but certainly not all, academic libraries have a category of paid borrowers that may include alumni, graduate students from other schools, professional people (lawyers, businessmen and women), individual scholars or free-lance writers, and corporations and associations. The library has the least claim on these individuals' lives, and yet some of them may be very active and responsible borrowers. Alumni often feel that because they attended the school they have an unquestionable right to the collection or because they have already contributed through the annual fund-raising event, they should get free privileges. They may still feel this way even if they get a significantly reduced rate. Others in this group are extremely appreciative and so grateful to be able to borrow at all from *any* academic library that they cheerfully pay the fee. Further, some of this group may not even live locally, and this may affect their use of the collection and their prompt or late return of materials.

Privileges for this group usually include borrowing for the length of the student loan or the shortest loan period and the ability to use the collection on weekends, when some libraries restrict access. The fee paid covers privileges for six months or a year, and unaffiliated borrowers are subject to the same fine charges for late or recalled books. Borrowing privileges are rescinded not only when the maximums for overdue books, fines, and billed books have been reached, but also if an expired card is not renewed. Since the library has no internal hold over these individuals when there are serious problems, the standard recourse, after the normal series of notices has been sent, is to refer the person to a collection agency or service. This action will get some results, but many times an individual has moved and left no record of a forwarding address. Dealing with this type of borrower can be most frustrating, and the efforts to contact the person, let alone get the books back, may be fruitless. Efforts to contact someone may go on for years and years. Meanwhile, the library is without those titles in its collection, and when a decision is finally made to replace them, they may no longer be available in print.

These aspects of dealing with outside borrowers may make some libraries question the value of offering such privileges, even at a high cost. Undoubtedly, there is a positive PR benefit for the alumni group in being able to obtain library privileges, even for a price. There may also be special reciprocal arrangements between two neighboring institutions. If neither group of users abuses the privilege, this can be good for inter-institutional relations. One has to be aware, however, of whom one allows to register for these privileges; without some screening, it is quite possible for the likes of James Shinn to qualify as an independent scholar and legitimately register for a card. This is a good time to question any address that is not a local one. Aside from the drawbacks of the unknown and the non-resident, unaffiliated borrowers are probably not that much worse about overdues than students and faculty/staff borrowers; the difference is that the consequences of their not returning their books on time or at all are greater for the library.

ON-LINE SYSTEMS

Living in the age of library automation, one may well say, "We've come a long way, baby." This is particularly true for the circulation department, which in many libraries was the second department (after cataloging), if not the first, to be automated. Circulation librarians today know more about what material is out, who has it out, how much money in fines that person owes, how many times a given book has gone out, how long that book has been out, and who wants it next. On-line circulation systems provide this additional information and consequently allow a far greater degree of control over material in the collection. One still wonders, nonetheless, if libraries, and academic libraries in particular, are really that much more successful at getting material back. Without a doubt, online systems offer a myriad of reports and tactics for managing the flow of material. Included are some items already mentioned: regular overdue notices, bill notices with replacement costs included, recall notices, book available notices, fines calculated for each patron, lists of everything a given patron has out, statistics on circulation by type of patron, and automatic suspension of borrowing privileges. Even with all these tools, it is probably a fact of human nature that as long as books circulate, some of them will be returned late or not at all. The options available for dealing with overdue materials are after all relatively few in number, and even with online systems, a large amount of staff time is required to process the patron information and make the necessary referrals. One hopes that strict loan policies actually result in more material being returned on time. Even if that is not the case, however, librarians should take some comfort in the suggestion that they probably know better where their material is than they did before automation.

REFERENCES

1. Robert Goehlert, "The Effect of Loan Policies on Circulation Recalls," *Journal of Academic Librarianship* 5 (May 1979): 80.
2. Ibid.

Outfoxing Overdues
in the Hospital Library

Patty Powell

ABSTRACT. Librarians in the small, special library can deal with overdues by knowing their users, being creative in reminding patrons about overdue materials, and outfoxing users while maintaining a sense of humor.

Recently an article was published in the *Bulletin of the Medical Library Association* about overdues and fines in academic health sciences libraries.[1] However, the vast majority of health sciences librarians are not academic; the smaller hospital, medical/insurance association, and medical/drug corporation libraries outnumber the academics. How do these smaller libraries view the problem of overdue materials?

Most hospital libraries do not see overdues as a major problem. First of all, the "meat" of medical and hospital information is found in journals published within the last five years, and most hospital libraries do not circulate journals. Instead, there are extensive photocopy services. (More and more, relevant medical articles are photocopied and attached to patient charts so the entire patient care team has access to the same information.) Secondly, many of the library users are on the hospital payroll and paychecks can be held or garnished until the overdues are returned. Physicians who are not on the payroll may be denied certain hospital privileges until they settle with the library. And thirdly, my experience as network librarian with twenty-one rural hospitals during the last seven years shows that "theft" and mutilation problems are far more serious than overdues.

The "theft" of materials usually results from absent-mindedness

Patty Powell, Extension Librarian, University of Kentucky, Lexington, KY 40506.

77

or laziness on the part of the user, who forgets to check out the material. This stems from the fact that the hospital library is accessible twenty-four hours a day but only staffed eight hours a day at the most. Most of the "stolen" materials eventually get back to the library (sometimes with a little prompting from the librarian to the most likely user). Mutilation occurs when books are chained to counters or tables, and the user is unable to take the needed book to a photocopier or to the site of a medical emergency. In my experience, torn-out pages are never returned. In this type of environment, overdue materials are viewed as a relatively lesser problem. However, every hospital librarian does face overdues problems, too. For the benefit of all hospital users, and eventually for the benefit of hospital patients, the librarian should be successful in limiting and retrieving overdue materials.

KNOW THY USER

The first consideration in overcoming an overdues problem is "know thy user"; second, be creative in your pursuit of the perpetrator; and last, sprinkle your pursuit with humor. Think of the collection of overdue materials as a challenge—perhaps as a challenging reference question! Did the overdue perpetrator perhaps return the book to the wrong library, or forget it in the on-call room, or loan it to a visiting student? Help the user remember where he left it, when he or she has looked everywhere at home and at the office and cannot find it.

To "know thy user" is a relatively easy task in a rural hospital. A hospital librarian with an outgoing personality usually knows each hospital staff member personally. There are only a few staff members in each medical department, and most departments are housed in the same building as the library (with possibly one or two hospital satellite clinics offsite). Therefore if a pathology text is missing or overdue it can usually be found in the pathology department, the morgue, or the laboratory lounge or restroom area. In some instances, the missing or overdue pathology text turns up in the school library of a hospital employee's son or daughter who is doing a senior project on a particular microbe. So, in addition to knowing thy user, it is smart to know thy fellow librarians in the community.

Knowledge of the library user helps the hospital librarian in planning a good service program. The better the library service program fits actual needs, the smaller the overdues problem will be. Make it easy for people to follow the library rules, and most of them will. First of all, establish a loan period that is reasonable enough to serve the needs of the majority of the primary library clientele. Then, if possible, allow telephone renewals. Also provide an in-house photo-copy service; often, a patron only keeps or renews a book because he wants access to a particular chart or chapter—not the whole book. If the library is not centrally located in the institution, have a book drop near the parking lot door (either inside or outside). Make sure there is a convenient way to check out or return materials in the library for second and third shift staff—and publicize it! If the hospital regularly trains a group of nursing students from the local college in operating room skills, either have multiple copies of operation room nursing texts or audiovisuals available, or set up a reserve system for these materials.

CREATIVITY

Creativity—this can be an enjoyable part of overdues prevention and retrieval. In one hospital library, when overdues got uncharac-teristically out of hand, a model of a human skeleton was hung by its thumbs with a sign around its neck reading, "I brought back my books three weeks late." Another library sends out a cartoon over-dues notice picturing a man with a dunce cap on his head, with the words "You blew it; your library books (book titles) are overdue." When the library patron has no idea where he left the book but knows it is somewhere in the hospital, one hospital library submits this ad to the monthly hospital calendar/bulletin:

> We will put a light in the window for
> the return of the missing _____
> If you notice it misshelved, let us know.

In addition to creative signs and notices, also be creative in your hunt for overdue or lost materials. A veteran hospital librarian gave me this hint—always look in the physicians restroom for overdue or missing materials. And, yes, I have found a few there!

Be creative in reminding people before the material is overdue. When they check out a book, verbally tell them the due date; this may jog their memory to tell you that they will be out of town that week and so request an extended loan period. If the user at the checkout is a student rotating through the hospital, ask him or her what the last day of rotation is. Or keep student rotation schedules (which can be provided by the personnel department) posted at the circulation desk. Never provide a due date longer than the hospital rotation.

Occasionally I have found that long-overdue materials (on the topics of childbirth, breastfeeding, and early childcare) that were charged out by physicians or nurses were given to patients. This can be prevented by working with the local public library. The hospital librarian might recommend certain titles that the physicians mention to patients. Or the hospital librarian might provide the latest hospital statistics on the local birthrate to help the public librarian justify an increase in the budget for those materials. The hospital librarian might also hand out public library brochures to new hospital employees to let them know about health materials available at the public library. Consider persuading the hospital administration to start or enhance its own patient education program. Hospitals are very competitive these days, and a good childbirth or childcare education program can be a real drawing-card for new patients.

THE GOOD HUMOR OVERDUES COLLECTOR

A sense of humor is a much-needed trait for hospital librarians, for there will always be at least one library user with a chronic overdues problem. Undoubtedly, he, if it is a man, will be the same physician who wears one black and one brown sock; his assistant is always tracking down his lost stethoscope, and the medical records personnel are always hunting for his misplaced records. Otherwise, this physician is very competent and has excellent rapport with his patients and colleagues. What to do? Outfox him! Offer to deliver a book to his office, even if he is there in the library asking for the book. Explain to him that you know he has several patients to see this morning and that you will help him by taking the book to his secretary. (Do this as discreetly as possible so that others don't expect the same service.) Get to know this physician's spouse. Obviously, the spouse must combat the same problem at home; so get the spouse to be your ally. Offer to remind the doctor about important dinner engagements with the spouse, and the spouse will offer to put overdue library materials in the physician's car when he leaves for the hospital. Where there's a will, there's a way! Believe me, the extra time it takes to know one's users pays off later. The spouse of the forgetful physician could be next year's president of the Medical Auxilliary—lo and behold, the money raised by their annual bake sale or fashion show might be donated to the hospital library!

So don't despair if you too must deal with overdues. Think, be challenged, be creative, and laugh a little. Your overdues problem may lead you to better opportunities. It is an opportunity to get to know your users a little better or the public library staff or your users' spouses. An overdues problem can also be translated into ammunition to justify duplicate copies of heavily used items, a new photocopy machine, or a new patient education library service. Open your eyes to the larger picture.

REFERENCE

1. Amy Gische Lyons, "Circulation Policies, Overdues, and Fines: Results of a Survey of Academic Health Sciences Libraries," *Bulletin of the Medical Library Association* 69 (July 1981): 326-329.

Managing Overdues
in the School Library

Wilma H. Bates

ABSTRACT. The article examines the overdues procedures of a high school library that uses a microcomputer to assist in the process. School system regulations and library policies are outlined. A microcomputer is used to maintain lists of students with overdue materials. Through automatic sorting and updating of files, the time required to maintain overdue files has been cut in half.

The management of overdues in public school libraries is usually regulated by local school board policies, with the procedures determined and supervised by the media specialist in each school. The method of dealing with the return of overdue materials at Greensboro's Page High School is probably similar to that used in most schools, with the exception of our use of the microcomputer.

The systemwide regulations we must follow in handling overdues are as follows:

SECTION 1. RATIONALE

1. Every student in the Greensboro Public School System should have easy and equal access to a wide range of materials in a variety of formats chosen to meet different levels of maturity, ability, and interest.
2. Students who keep materials beyond designated loan periods or lose or damage materials deny other students the use of these materials.

Wilma H. Bates, Media Specialist, Walter Hines Page Senior High School, Greensboro, NC 27405.

SECTION 2. PRINCIPLES

1. Fines will not be charged for overdue materials in any Greens-boro Public School K-12.
2. Damaged and/or lost materials will be paid for in accordance with the established individual school policy governing other lost or damaged school properties.
3. Overdue materials at the beginning of a semester shall be considered "lost material."
4. Procedures for collecting monies owed for lost or damaged materials shall follow those for any other school fee (Board Policy JBCBAA (JSA)—"Collection of Board Approved Student Fees").

SECTION 3. ROLES AND RESPONSIBILITIES

1. Media Specialist
   A. Establishes and maintains fair and liberal loan policies.
   B. Notifies students of overdue materials through one or more of the following:

   > (1) personal contact
   > (2) overdue notices (multiple overdue notices supplied by Media Department)
   > (3) lists to teachers
   > (4) notices to parents (after students have had ample opportunity to return materials)

   C. Requires students to return overdue materials before "checking out" other materials. However, the students retain the privilege of coming to the media center and using materials in the center.
   D. Encourages the care and return of materials in a variety of ways, e.g., teaching proper care of materials; convenient materials return boxes; announcements; supervised locker checks; etc.
   E. Keeps the principal informed, as appropriate, of students who have overdue materials or who have lost or damaged materials.
2. The Teacher
   A. Works with students in the individual classroom on the care and return of all school owned materials.

3. The Principal
    A. Interprets the "Overdue/Lost/Damaged Media Center Materials, K-12" policy to staff and parents in the individual school.
    B. Implements the procedures outlined in the Board of Education Policies.[1]

Most school media specialists agree that a liberal circulation policy encourages students to check out materials properly and discourages theft and mutilation of materials. We have no restriction on the amount of materials students may check out. Circulation and overdue policies for students at our school are as follows:

> Books are loaned to students for a three-week period. The date due is stamped when materials are checked out. Books not on request may be renewed. Overdue notices are sent to students through their homerooms. Students should write first and last name and homeroom on the circulation card for everything checked out. Students with overdue materials may not check out anything. The media center does not charge fines. Students are expected to return materials on time and to pay for lost or damaged materials. Reference books, reserve books, information file materials, magazines, and audiovisual materials may be checked out overnight. These materials are checked out at the end of the day and are due in the media center before the homeroom period of the following school day. Special arrangements may be made for students to check out equipment.[2]

Circulation and overdue policies do not apply to teachers. Our school has a faculty of eighty-five, who borrow materials and equipment from the media center for as long as needed. They are cooperative about returning materials when requested by others; they do tend to keep materials out a long time when not reminded about them. At the end of the school year, we ask teachers to return everything for inventory.

Since it is not standard procedure for school media centers to send information about overdues for systemwide or state-level reports, we have no records available for comparing our situation with other schools or noting increases or decreases in overdues from year to year. We can only make estimates. Our media center serves 1,465 students and circulates approximately 1,000 books and many other materials to these students each month. We estimate that about one-third of the materials checked out by students are not returned on time. At the end of each semester, about 15 percent of our students are on the overdue list. A small percentage of our students never return or pay for materials.

The amount of money collected for lost and damaged materials (about $200 each year) is not sufficient to replace losses. Students pay the original cost of the item, not adjusted for inflation, processing costs, or condition. We stress to students that we would much rather have the materials than their money. If students find books after they pay for them, the school returns their money if they produce the receipt for payment.

Diplomas are held for graduating seniors who owe the school for anything, including library materials. There are really no consequences for students who withdraw from school with overdue books. (About two hundred students withdraw from our school each year.) Withdrawing students are supposed to clear with us before they leave the school. If they do withdraw still owing materials, we write a letter to their parents about the need to return materials. We estimate that success occurs with about half of these letters. We also forward the information to their new schools, if the students are transferring. If we get such information about new students at our school, we add their names to our overdue list and do not allow them to check out materials until they return overdue materials to their former schools.

Since returning library material on time is not a top-priority item for most high school students, we use several strategies to promote the return of materials. First of all, we teach students about being responsible library users, a task common to all school media centers. At the beginning of the school year we have orientation sessions for new students with a slide show we have prepared to explain our media center's policies and procedures. We also put up posters and displays to remind students about the proper care of materials and the importance of returning them on time. At times, such as during National Library Week, we give away prizes (usually paperback books) with the stipulation that students must have a clear record (no overdues at that time) to be eligible to win. All during the year, teachers help out by collecting and returning books when students have completed assignments using library materials. Some teachers will even require the return of materials as part of the assignment. In spite of such efforts, we have to remind many students about returning overdues.

The need for the prompt return of materials borrowed for overnight use is most urgent and requires the use of personal contact for immediate results. Because these materials do need to be in the media center during the school day, we stress at check-out time that the students may take these materials home overnight only if they make a sincere commitment to return them at the beginning of the next school day. Usually students cooperate. They know that many libraries do not allow materials such as reference books and magazines to circulate, and they appreciate having the opportunity to check them out. Each morning we check the special notebook where we record overnight loans and send student assistants (our SWAT force) to students and request (demand!) the return of materials. We continue daily personal contact plus written notices until overnight loans are returned.

We send written notices to students beginning about one week after any materials are due. This time-consuming task is handled almost entirely by our full-time aide. Student assistants do not help with this task. We think that the high degree of accuracy we maintain causes students to take our notices seriously. We do not want to devote any more time to the job than absolutely necessary, but we do feel that it deserves careful attention. Our aide does take the time to check the shelves to be sure that we do not send notices for books that are on the shelves without the circulation card.

This year we have increased the efficiency of dealing with overdues by using a microcomputer. Our aide used to spend almost two days each week working on overdues; now she spends less than one.

The media center does not have its own microcomputer, but we do have access to an Apple IIe with two disk drives and a dot matrix printer. This equipment belongs to the computer lab and is used for instruction. We need only about two hours at a computer each week to enter data and print, and it is easy to schedule this time around student use.

Because we did not have sufficient funds to buy software designed for specific library functions, we selected a data management program, Personal Filing System or PFS (Software Publishing), that is easily used for a variety of purposes. (In addition to using this program for overdues, we use it for making lists such as our magazine subscriptions and new books.)

To use PFS for managing overdues, we enter the following information from the card for each overdue book: student's name and homeroom, call number, accession number, author, title, price, and date due of the overdue material. This information is saved on a disk, copied onto a back-up disk, and stored in a locked cabinet. (This precaution prevents our students who are computer "whiz kids" from having access to the information and possibly "playing" with it.)

Entering this information requires about the same amount of typing time as our previous procedure with individual notices, but in the overall process for dealing with overdues, the microcomputer saves a great deal of time. It eliminates the time required to insert individual multiple-part notices into a typewriter, remove them, and separate the copies. It allows for easy correction of mistakes. (No more carbon paper and messy erasing!) The information entered can be sorted and listed however we want it, so we do not need to do any sorting or filing. Our aide used to spend a great deal of time sorting the cards so that all the overdues for one student could be typed on one notice. Then the cards would require refiling by classification for ease in checking in materials.

The microcomputer also allows for easy updating of the overdue files. The process of deleting information for returned overdues is simple, requiring only a few keystrokes. The updating is done once each week just before entering new data. Our previous system required the clearing of two separate files (located in different areas of the media center) when students returned overdues.

Once it is entered, the information is used in a variety of ways without the need to retype anything. Each week we have the computer print a list (sorted by homerooms) of students with overdues. We photocopy this list for all the teachers; it replaces the individual notices we used to send. One advantage of this computer-produced list is that the information accumulates from one week to the next, so students are regularly reminded about all overdues until they return them. With our previous system, we sent one original and only two copies to students. Often students mistakenly assumed that their library record was clear when they no longer received overdue notices. Another advantage is that the list is sent to all the teachers. Although only the homeroom teachers are directly responsible for notifying students about overdues, other teachers (such as coaches and club advisors) who have special influence with some students can and do help with the return of overdue materials. Since the teachers post the list rather than give out individual notices, we want to protect the students' right to privacy, and we do not print titles of overdue materials on this list.

When we planned using the microcomputer for overdues, we thought we would not send individual notices because it is easier to print lists than individual forms. We discovered that a printout with sufficient spacing is easy to cut apart for individual notices, and decided that it is not too time-consuming to prepare individual notices once each grading period. We ask teachers to hand these to students or to attach them to report cards. This additional notice is of particular benefit to students who do not attend homeroom regularly.

We print another list (in alphabetical order by the names of the students) to keep at the circulation desk. It replaces a rotary file previously used to check for students with overdues when they were checking out books and AV materials. (Maintenance of this file was another typing chore.) Student assistants at the circulation desk are responsible for reminding students that they must return their overdues before checking out anything else. We find that assistants find it easier to check a list than to look into a file, so they now do this checking more consistently.

A computer printout with the names of students with overdue materials is posted by our main entrance and is an additional way of communicating with students about overdue materials that we did not have in our previous procedures. In order to attract the students' attention to this list, we have illustrated the poster with cartoons about overdue books.

In addition to notifying students weekly about overdues, we make a special effort at the end of each semester to get materials back to the media center. We send letters to parents of students with overdue materials, informing them about the policy of prohibiting students with overdues from enrolling in school the next semester. If we do not get a positive response from these letters, we make telephone calls. We also compile a list for the principal and assistant principals of all students who have not cleared at the end of the semester. This list used to require another large sorting and typing task, but now we can produce it by computer in a matter of minutes.

The principal and assistant principals are very supportive in assisting with the return of materials to the media center. They encourage teachers to stress to students the importance of being responsible about all school obligations. The principals have conferences with many of the students who owe materials to the library.

They see to it that library materials found in lockers are returned to us. The principal warns students that they may not enroll in school for the next semester if they have obligations, but this policy is not rigidly enforced. He must deal with each student on an individual basis and consider financial conditions and extenuating circumstances.

We do not yet know to what extent our new method of dealing with overdues is more effective than our previous system was. Two-thirds of the way into the fall semester we have sent notices on 840 overdues. At this time 205 students have overdues totaling $1,304.72. So we still have a problem with overdues, but think the increased communication has helped alleviate it. We have not observed a reaction recently reported in an article about new technology in school media centers, "In Shaker Heights the students are excited about getting overdue notices, says Stepanian. The image of the library changes immediately with printouts."[3] We do know that the new system is much more efficient; we are saving a lot of time. Any time saved from the time-consuming but necessary task of handling overdues is a real benefit to the entire school media program.

REFERENCES

1. Greensboro Public Schools, "Overdue/Lost/Damaged Media Center Materials K-12," *Systemwide Administrative Regulation JS-R* (1979).

2. Page Senior High, *Student-Parent Handbook, 1983-84* (Greensboro, N.C.:Phyl, 1983).

3. "How Are School Libraries Doing With Automating Circulation Systems?" in "Readers' Queries," *School Library Media Quarterly* 12 (Fall 1983): 59.

Overdues Procedures Using a Microcomputer

Willie Nelms

ABSTRACT. A medium-sized public library has applied micro-computer technology to the problem of overdues. A file of patrons with overdue materials is maintained, and the computer produces bills and Rolodex cards (for a delinquent patrons file). Savings are estimated at $1200 annually.

Overdue books and overdues notices are as old as the lending of public library material. The preparation of overdue notices for patrons is a time-consuming, costly, and thankless task. As surely as patrons borrow material, some will fail to return material. For this reason, the necessity of preparing overdue notices will continue as long as libraries lend books.

Because overdue notice preparation is such a routine, yet necessary, task, it is advisable to make it as systematic and efficient as possible. The advent of the microcomputer offers many small and medium-sized libraries an opportunity to improve the effectiveness of their overdues procedures. These powerful machines give libraries that cannot afford full-scale automated circulation systems a chance to use computer technology.

With the microcomputer, costs can be reduced for almost all libraries. In a curious twist of fate, the combining of the latest in technology with one of the oldest problems in the profession can contribute to overall library efficiency.

Sheppard Memorial Library, serving the 92,000 residents of Pitt County, North Carolina, is one library that has applied microcomputer technology to the problems of overdues. Sheppard is a medium-sized library with 125,000 volumes and 20,000 borrowers, who are served through five public service desks.

The annual circulation of the library system in 1982-1983 was

Willie Nelms, Director, Sheppard Memorial Library, Greenville, NC 27834.

268,900. A manual Gaylord circulation system is used by the library. Loans are made for a three-week period, and overdue notices are sent out when books are four weeks overdue. This notice, providing the replacement cost of the overdue material, tells the patron that only an overdue fee will be charged if the items are returned. Fines are 5 cents per day per item, with a $2.00 maximum.

Over the years, the library has consistently found that 3.5 percent of the material borrowed requires sending a first overdue notice. On average, each overdue notice contains two and one half items.

At the point of the first overdue statement, a Rolodex card containing the information pertinent to the delinquency is prepared for each public service desk. Patrons may not borrow anything until all overdue material is returned and all fines are paid. A patron's name is checked against the Rolodex file whenever a loan is made.

When material is eight weeks overdue, a second notice is sent to the patron. This is a bill with a strongly worded letter advising patrons that it is illegal to retain library material and threatening legal action. Approximately 1 percent of all items circulated require such notices.

Until January 1983, all notices in the library system were prepared manually. Each desk (except in the Main Library adult and children's areas) prepared its own notices and generated five copies of Rolodex cards. Notices for the two Main Library desks were prepared by the same clerical staff.

This process involved pulling the overdue book cards from the circulation well for the week to be billed. These cards were collated by the patron's registration number, and the patron information was manually searched in the cross-reference registration book. At this point an overdue notice was typed, including the patron's name and address, as well as the information identifying the book. The replacement cost of the book was also provided, and the value of all the material was totaled at the bottom of the bill.

At this point the Rolodex cards were prepared for each public service desk. Even using carbons, two typings of each record were required to generate enough Rolodex cards. The creation of second notices required a clerk to check the circulation well for the appropriate dates and to go through a process similar to that for the first bills.

Prior to the introduction of the microcomputer, approximately twenty hours per week were expended at the various desks in order to generate overdue notices. The growing circulation of the library system brought home to the staff the need for a more effective means of preparing overdue notices.

The library has a three-year registration period. Periodically, the registration files are purged of expired cards. Since February 1982, all registrations have been entered into the microcomputer, eliminating the need for the cross-reference registration book necessary with the Gaylord manual circulation system.

At the time it was decided to use the microcomputer in overdues preparation, slightly over 8,000 registered borrowers were in the computer files. This sizable body of 40 percent of the registered borrowers provided a good base for the preparation of overdues via computer.

With the advent of computer assistance, it was possible to centralize overdues notice preparation in the library system. This offered greater consistency in overdues procedures. The amount of time required to complete the overdues process decreased from twenty hours per week to fewer than twelve hours.

The step-by-step description given below details the various procedures followed with the use of the microcomputer and notes the marked changes from the totally manual process. It is vital to remember that this process does not claim to be an ''automated'' system. Instead, it is an application of powerful microcomputer technology to supplement manual procedures, making the preparation of notices more efficient. The steps include:

1. Book cards for the items to be billed are pulled from the circulation well of each desk and given to the overdues clerk each Monday.

2. A clerk enters the patron's registration number, the abbreviation of the branch where the item is overdue, and the date of the notice. Since CONDOR has an auto-repeat mode, the branch and date can be left in place for all notices until a change occurs. The author, title, and price of the book are entered at this point. The necessity of collating cards by registration number is eliminated, as the machine can pull this information together at the proper time.

3. The computer matches the patron's identification number in the overdue file with the patron information in the registration database. In fact, the first name, last name, address, city, state, and zip code are posted for each overdue item. This obviates the need to manually search for the patron information when the patrons are in the registration database.

4. If a patron is not in the registration database, the operator is given the number of the patrons not found. She then looks up these patrons manually and enters them in the registration database. This information is then posted to the overdues database. In this way, patrons with overdue items will never need to be searched manually after they are entered in the database. Considering the repeat nature of overdues offenses, this is a very attractive feature.

As of March 1984, 15,000 of the system's 20,000 registered borrowers are in the computer database, and fewer than 3 percent need to be searched manually in the registration books.

5. At this point, the overdue items are sorted and the bill is written by the computer. The value of each item is indicated on the bill, and the total value of the material is provided by the computer. The patron's name and address are written on the bill in a position to be displayed in a window envelope. No typing is required by the operator.

6. Having finished the overdues notice, the computer produces five copies of Rolodex cards. These cards contain the same information that was sent in the notice. Thus, there is no need to type Rolodex cards for the various desks.

7. The most time-consuming part of the entire task comes at this point. This is the separating of the pin-fed Rolodex cards. The task is boring, and requires a good deal of time. Compared to the typing time involved with the manual procedure, however, the trade-off is well worth the effort.

8. When items are returned and a record is completely cleared, the Rolodex card is withdrawn from the desk and sent to the Main Library. The returned items are eliminated from the database, and the computer generates a list of the patrons and material cleared. This eliminates the manual list preparation that was necessary before the introduction of the computer.

9. When it is time to generate second notices, the computer provides a list of the items still overdue at each desk. This is checked against the files of each facility and verified. The database is updated to show the actual delinquencies at this point, and the machine generates the second notices. This eliminates the manual typing of a second bill.

As mentioned earlier, the time saved in eliminating these manual overdues tasks is substantial.

Actual savings in terms of money are estimated to be $1200 annually. This takes into consideration the cost of supplies for the computer paper products, which are more expensive than those necessary for the manual process.

In addition to cost displacement, the database management system provides several by-products that are very useful and were not readily available in the manual process:

1. Because the price of each item is indicated in the database, the computer can provide statistics on the total value of overdue material for which bills have been sent out. This includes the number of items outstanding, as well as the maximum, minimum, and average value of each item.
2. The computer easily tabulates the number of items overdue at each desk and gives the cost of this material. With this information, the library staff can easily calculate return rates per desk and can measure the effectiveness of the overdues procedure.
3. With the computer capability of sorting the database by various fields, it is easy to find information on specific books and to identify categories of material outstanding.

It should be remembered that the storage medium is a ten-megabyte hard disk. The hard disk provides speed as well as sufficient storage capacity for the activities described above. Anyone contemplating a similar procedure should make certain that adequate storage capacity is available to perform such functions. Using floppy disks, incidentally, would be much more cumbersome and decidedly slower. The process described could not be accomplished in a library similar to Sheppard with fewer than 5,000,000 bytes of storage space.

In the final analysis, the microcomputer-based overdues system has provided real savings. While the time required to accomplish overdues preparations for the week is less than twelve hours, it should be remembered that some of this time (as much as 40 percent) involves the computer sorting, posting, and printing. During this time, it is not necessary for the operator to be at the machine. This time can be spent performing other library functions. The actual "hands on" time is closer to seven hours per week.

For these reasons, the use of the microcomputer in the preparation of overdues has proven to be a very effective process at this medium-sized public library. Other libraries may be encouraged to attempt similar applications of this technology.

Library Automation and Overdues:
A Discussion of Possibilities
and Potentialities

Patrick McClintock

ABSTRACT. The article is intended as a guide for libraries that are considering automation and for which the overdues process is an area of concern. Manual and automated overdues procedures are compared, and special features of automated systems (sorting by ZIP code, manual overrides) are examined. Minimum requirements for the automated handling of the overdues function are outlined. For example, such a system should be able to produce overdues notices in batch mode.

When a library makes the decision to implement an automated circulation system, certain judgments regarding its existing operation must be made; what activities will the new system be expected to handle, and how will routine practices related to these activities be adapted? As the self-scrutiny begins, an early warning often sounded concerns the need to rethink operations, and not simply transfer manual processes to a computerized system.

As policies and procedures tend to get streamlined with the advent of automation, so the tangles wrought by years of overlaid administrations and practices, both written and unwritten, tend to uncomplicate themselves. Possibilities of total inventory control and patron demographics make changing circulation policies more acceptable, perhaps easier to justify. But linked to circulation policies is an area that is so tied to local practices and attitudes that most developers make their automated systems conform to it—the generation and distribution of overdues.

Overdue notices—gentle reminders, matter-of-fact bills, telephone calls from a collection agency, pre-dawn visits by the Library

Patrick McClintock, Automation Project Manager, Lexington Public Library, Lexington, KY 40507.

97

Police—are a reality, perhaps distasteful to some, in most library systems. Whether a library sees its role as archival, instructional, informational, or recreational, once materials go out the door, the library is faced with the problem of how to get them back. More significantly, this effort is conducted at the personal level of the library/patron relationship. Whether patron responsibility is assumed or specified, a library must rely on a patron's sense of responsibility in whatever approach to overdues the library takes.

A library that chooses to generate and deliver (or have delivered) notices and bills regarding overdue library materials operates on the premise that the materials are worth recovering; how else justify the costs of the overdues process? A few libraries add handling costs to overdue fines when notices are sent; some libraries don't bother to send notices for materials like paperback books, figuring that replacement costs may be nearly equal to overdues processing costs. Yet the process was never meant to be cost-effective. Depending upon the personal attitudes of administrators and managers and upon prevailing community attitudes towards responsibility, libraries have instituted overdue fines/notices processes as systems have become too large to contact in person all patrons with overdue books to ask them to please return their books.

As with any policy, an overdue policy can be as complicated as an institution wants (or perhaps doesn't want) it to be. Special libraries and academic libraries, to use two familiar examples, may have several layers of enforcement or regulation built into overdues policy; it is often far easier to go after (and collect from) a student than a tenured faculty member, and a research assistant doesn't have the same privileges a corporate vice president has. It is apparent that, while these may be extreme or frivolous examples, a certain amount of sensitivity is connected with the overdues process. Applying policies consistently creates all kinds of political problems; but it is consistency that implementation of an automated system requires.

Complicated circulation policies are no problem for most automated library systems. You want a hundred different material types? You got 'em. Sixty branches? Piece of cake. Different fines for each day of the week? Color of book? Age of patron? The levels of detail exist for uncountable permutations and combinations. The same is true of procedures such as that used in the case of overdues. If a procedure can be broken into unique elements that can be expressed somehow in machine language, it can be made part of a library's automated system. Enforcement, however, creates certain problems that are easily handled in its less rigid analog version. Unless "told" beforehand, an automated system doesn't "recognize" the chairman of the board of library trustees or the college president. If the automated system begins to track their overdue materials, the chairman and the president will be treated as any other patron with overdues. Human intervention is required to make exceptions to rules implanted in operating systems or software modules.

Generally, circulation control modules of library system software packages create links between records in two files—a patron file and a bibliographic or item file. When a book is checked out, for example, and a due date recorded, the due date is found and usually displayed in both files. The due date is linked to the bibliographic record (in some cases to a shorter record that is a subset of the full cataloging record); and when the record is displayed, users of the automated system can determine the due date of materials whose status is shown as checked out or circulating.

Most automated systems provide for overriding set parameters, both in the circulation function and the overdues process. System operators at the proper security level can force the system to ignore in a sense the commands that are generated by overstepping parameters. But the system can still track the override; in most automated systems, part of the usual security activity includes recording the number of overrides performed by a staff person at specific work stations and for which patron. The override is also usually tracked in the patron record. The system reports on overrides on a regular basis, allowing for scrutiny of both system parameters and staff performance.

A manual overdues process can have many steps, routines, subroutines and end products. The following general outline describes one process: an item is checked out or charged, and a manual record is made of the transaction. This record, be it handwritten or a Hollerith card or photographic film, is stored in a file or files. A single file is usually an item file arranged in call number order, alphabetical order by author's last name, or the like. Secondary files may be in the form of alphabetical lists of patrons. At specific intervals, these files are searched for items that are still charged beyond the due date. Records are selected for processing. A snag list may be compared against the records, and the library's shelves checked for the items overdue. Records that survive this search are then typed on multipart notices. A final search of the shelves may be conducted before the notices are sent. When the notices are sent, one copy of the notice goes to a patron file, one copy to an item file in call number order, and perhaps one copy to an item file in transaction number order. The patron, of course, receives a copy.

Here is how an automated library system would handle these same steps. When an item is charged, a link between the item record in the database and the patron record in the database is created. This link is not broken until discharge. At a frequency predetermined by the library, the automated system searches the records (some systems search the patron records, some the item records, some the links) and determines which items are overdue. The system compares the records selected with the inventory file ("searches the shelves") as a check, and those items not found become the batch to be processed. Notices are printed using data from the item file/patron file, where the existence of the overdue notice itself is now also recorded.

When an item is checked out in an automated library system, it is "timed" by the internal clock of the system's central processor. Some libraries opt to tell their systems the time and date each time the system is started or a new business day begins; most rely on the computer to keep its own clock and calendar. When an item checked out two weeks ago is due today, for example, then tonight at 12:00:01 it will become overdue. If the item is returned today after the library closes, it won't be checked in until tomorrow—and it will be overdue. The automated system will duly note the fact and record the fine (if fines exist) in the patron's record. It is for this reason that a library may choose not to tell its system that it is a new day until overnight returns are checked in.

Another option for beating the internal clock is the grace period. If a one- or two-day grace is allowed on returns, most overnight returns can be checked in without fines being incurred by the borrower. Grace periods also help cover returns to branches or other agencies of the library system whose hours are not the same as those of the main library. Grace periods, however, introduce an element of inconsistency, as two days' grace in a two-week circulation period really creates a sixteen-day period.

Most automated systems are designed to produce overdue notices in batch mode during times of low central processor activity. Notices can usually be generated as frequently as a library system wants. Two or three notices are standard, with one notice in the form of a bill. If the notices are sent through the U.S. Postal Service, some systems can sort the notices into ZIP code order before printing. This feature is not available in all automated systems, but those that do not have it are sure to get it soon since reduced bulk mailing postal rates apply when ZIP code order is observed. Overdues can also be sorted and printed alphabetically on most systems.

If a library mails overdue notices, several possibilities are available. Multipart pin-feed mailers for printers with tractor devices are common. Card stock is used for notices that contain no privileged or sensitive information such as fine amounts.

It should be noted that if a library wants to generate notices and print them on a device attached to a central processor, that device cannot be the console printer used to communicate with the CPU. A separate printer is needed to print notices, as well as any other report or label. This frees the console device for communication, and prevents CPU commands and responses from showing up on notices.

Automated systems can also generate overdue notices in the standard multipart form that is inserted into envelopes.

Some automated systems can handle overnight returns at any time during operation. When an item is checked in (discharged), the operating system can be set in a mode that bypasses the internal system clock. A staff person must decide if the item being discharged meets the requirements for the operation.

One problem created by generating and printing overdue notices is related to timeliness. If the notices are not sent the same day that they are printed, an item returned that day will continue to accumulate fines, or the patron will get a notice for the returned item. In the future, some systems will make one last check of materials for which notices are to be sent to determine that the materials have not in fact been returned.

Some systems do not allow for a grace period, especially when the system is designed for special or academic libraries with extended circulation periods such as semesters. For the most part, a grace period is still an extension of the circulation period. What the patron believes to be the circulation period and what the system is told the period is can be two different things.

If a library charges fines for overdue materials, it may notice an increase in fines collected after it implements an automated circulation system. Although fines do not prevent overdues, and although notices sent in a timely manner may decrease the number of days overdue material is kept, the accurate logging of fines and the inability of automated systems to forgive fines usually means an increase in the dollar amount due to a lending library. A library can choose to bill patrons on a regular basis for the nickel-dime fines that gradually accumulate. In either case, it is the library's decision as to whether to collect the amount due or forgive the fine(s). Thus a decision may be made to forgive a ten-cent fine when an item is returned. In an automated system, on the other hand, the forgiveness is on a larger scale: one large absolution replaces many small ones.

Certain functions of automated circulation systems related to overdue materials can be considered minimum requirements for a good working system. Charges should be recorded in both the patron and item files of the system. The discharge function should allow for overnight returns (if not overdue) to be checked in without penalty. Grace periods, unless so thoroughly entrenched as to be sacred, should be abandoned or built into the circulation period. Automated systems should be able to generate overdue notices in batch mode during low processor activity; generation should be at any desired frequency or on demand if necessary. The system should print notices in the form preferred by the library: multipart mailers, cardstock or separate pages inserted into envelopes. Notices should be sorted in ZIP code order to obtain the reduced U.S. Postal Service rate (other sorts should be possible for other methods of distribution such as campus mail or interoffice mail). The system should "search" for overdue items within the library one final time before generating notices. Various reports on overdues (not just the number sent) should be available for analysis, documentation, or policy justification.

At no time in the generation process should manual intervention be required until notices have been printed and must be removed from the printer to the mail or distribution point.

It was originally intended in this article to compare the methods employed by existing automated library systems in generating overdue notices and bills. Because of time constraints, however, a complete survey of existing systems was not possible. In fairness to those not polled, no specific systems have been mentioned or described. It is hoped that this discussion is not too general or vague. Rather let it be viewed as a guide for libraries considering automation and for whom the overdues process presents one area of concern. There are many similarities among automated systems in methods of processing and generating overdue notices and bills. For the information and opinions contained in this discussion the author has relied on descriptions provided by representatives of automated systems, first-hand knowledge of several systems, and empirical and actual knowledge of overdues processing.

The Fines—No Fines Debate

Barbara Anderson

ABSTRACT. Advocates of fines for overdue materials see fines as an incentive for returning materials on time, as a display of the library's seriousness about its rules, and as an income generator. Several libraries have reported success in returning to fines after no-fines experiments. On the other side, those advocating the elimination of fines argue that fines do not make a significant difference in a library's overdues, that they are a hardship to children, that they cost more to administer than they bring in, and that they damage the library's image. The author suggests that individual librarians must decide for themselves about fines.

Librarians who administer circulating collections are searching for the best response to borrowers who return materials after the due date and who sometimes even treat the materials borrowed as their own personal collections. One public librarian has asserted that some people have virtual libraries of their own consisting of unreturned public library materials.[1] Late return of books and book loss are severe problems. The constant replacing of unreturned materials is an unbearable burden for libraries with already strained book budgets. Librarians are disconcerted by an apparent disregard of community values which are basic and assumed in the library's lending operation.

It is common for libraries to charge fines for infringements of their borrowing rules. Library fines are a library tradition. The threat of a fine provides the patron with an incentive for returning materials on time, a penalty for returning materials late, and an education in being a responsible citizen. It is claimed that fines rep-

Barbara Anderson, Head, East Winston Branch, Forsyth County Public Library, Winston-Salem, NC 27101.

resent a correct posture for librarians to take in response to the generally irresponsible character of our society. Fines, moreover, provide a show of the library's seriousness about its rules and regulations as well as some small amount of income.[2]

Within the past five years, *Library Journal* has consistently characterized the library attitude toward overdues policies in the same way. Libraries have been described as questioning their lenient overdues policies and deciding to become increasingly strict. In the recent reports of libraries' responses to high overdues rates, it has been the report of the "tough" approach that predominates.[3]

Certainly the advocates of fines believe deeply in goals that few could fault. A community college librarian claims that the whole point of his library's strong fines policy is "to have the books optimally available (on the shelf) except when they are already being used. . .We do not consider a book sitting on someone's desk or in the back seat of a car for three months as use."[4] The Pennsylvania State Library director claims that by virtue of his library's system of fines, instituted after 225 years without fines, the library has "become more people-oriented by permitting more users to gain better access to more books."[5]

Libraries reporting that their return to a fines policy was a wise, successful choice persuade us that fines are a strong incentive for the prompt return of books. The Alpha Park (Illinois) Public Library tried a virtually fine-free policy for six months, only to find that overdues increased from 2½ percent to 9 percent of total circulation. The library, with no misgivings, returned to fines, and, as a consequence, overdues returned to the former 2 percent level.[6] The library in Sudbury, Massachusetts, found that during its no-fines experiment book return dropped from 96 percent to 80 percent and caused a tripling of the number of overdue notices sent. The library returned to a policy of fines, and book return rose to the former level, a respectable 96 percent of total materials borrowed.[7]

Firmly fixed in the public mind is the idea that fines are a proper punishment for patrons who have not honored their obligation to return books on time. The public library in Richmond, Indiana, dropped its no-fines policy not only because it failed to accomplish its primary goal, an anticipated decrease in overdue materials, but because patrons actually objected to it. The public felt that the discipline encouraged by fines was needed. Patrons felt guilty about not paying fines for their abuses of library privileges.[8]

It can be argued, very practically, that fines are obviously valuable because they are a source of revenue for the library. Even though the amount of revenue is small, some feel that even the smallest amount should be welcomed. In fact, the King County (Washington) Library boasted of the huge increase in receipts from overdue and lost books that followed the raising of fines from five cents to ten cents per day and the intervention of a collection agency to collect from patrons who owed more than $15.[9]

Some believe that fines are a good educational tool. Fines teach people, especially young people, to be responsible and to respect others' rights, public property, and rules and regulations. The underlying assumption of this view is that public libraries should be involved in this teaching because they are, first and foremost, educational institutions. Some school librarians, but by no means all of them, also find particular merit in the argument that fines teach responsibility.[10]

Librarians have written about the rough, uncaring world and have argued that library fines are a sensible, responsible measure for the guardians of commonly owned books to take. The Enoch Pratt Free Library, in the early seventies, a difficult time for many of the large urban libraries, attributed its many overdues to "an apparent increase in irresponsibility which seems to characterize the times."[11] A Memphis Public Library spokesman described the attitude of some library patrons this way: "We'll bring back books when we are good and ready, they are as much mine as yours. Sue me."[12] The director of the Pennsylvania State Library referring to a complete lack of consideration by researchers and students described his own very strong feelings on the matter:

> If you believe that all people are basically honest, charitable toward others, cooperative, you could also believe a system of library fines to be unnecessary. However, if you believe, as I do, that there is always a sizeable minority of the citizenry who is fundamentally dishonest, selfish, and careless, then a system of library fines becomes essential.[13]

Librarians have responded to high overdues rates by returning to fines, increasing fines, imposing service charges, taking legal action against offending patrons, asking the mayor to help, and, in general, going to all lengths to recover unreturned materials and the costs of recovering them. We read that the Union College Library, in Schenectady, is adamant about its one-year loan period for faculty and will try everything conceivable to enforce it, including the usual reminder notices, hand-written notes, phone calls, and visits—in other words, a virtual assault on violators of its rules.[14] Harvard University has adopted a steep penalty schedule, which includes a $15 fine for materials more than five weeks overdue.[15] The Jervis Public Library in Rome, New York, was so proud of its success in taking legal action against delinquent patrons that its director has offered, for a mere $10, a kit of forms and instructions for taking patrons to court.[16] Especially in the last few years, most librarians report that they are communicating to their patrons their utter seriousness about the rules of borrowing in their libraries.

So why would a library choose to eliminate fines? In the early seventies, there was a marked trend for libraries to consider a no-fines policy. It was claimed that fines do not make a significant difference in a library's overdues, that they in fact deter the ultimate return of some materials and work an unfair hardship on children and the typical "nonusers" for whom we design our outreach programs, that they cost more to administer than the amount of revenue realized, that they damage the library's image and have a detrimental effect on the library's total circulation.[17]

The most detailed study in support of a no-fines policy and the most detailed study of fines in general is Robert S. Meyer's study of the Alameda County (California) Library System's no-fines experiment. The experiment was undertaken expressly because so much clerical time (a full 15 percent of each branch clerk's time) was spent on fine-related activities. The Alameda Library centralized its overdues operations and one of the most immediate results of the experiment was *increased circulation*. Patrons were much more likely to check out many books. The library staff felt that in general patrons who returned materials promptly when there were fines still returned promptly and delinquent borrowers were, of course, still delinquent. Although the staff admits that without fines there may be more slightly overdue books, they maintain that more books are returned.[18]

Many feel that children suffer unfairly from a policy of fines. Often children have no control over when their books are returned. Children, especially poor ones, who incur fines may be forbidden from using the library again by their parents. Certainly it is not desirable for young patrons to feel that "there is a Cain's Mark of the Unpaid Fine on their foreheads."[19] An important aim of Enoch Pratt's experiment with eliminating fines for children's books was to give poor children unable to pay fines and children who had been forbidden by their parents to use the library a chance to borrow library materials without fear of incurring a fine. An essential part of the Enoch Pratt experiment was an intensive effort at explaining to children exactly what their privileges and obligations were.[20]

The implementation of a fines policy will inevitably involve some kind of inequity. Fines are a more burdensome kind of punishment for the disadvantaged than for the typical middle-class library patron. John Berry contends that fines, because they deny access to people unable to pay them, violate the Library Bill of Rights.[21] Fines are unfairly levied on "good library patrons" whose failure to return materials promptly was for good reason. Or perhaps the circulation staff uses discretion, favoritism in the eyes of some, in the assessing of fines.[22]

In a report on the Carroll (Iowa) Public Library, which has always had fines, Gordon Wade concludes from its no-fines experiment that although there are more overdues when there are no fines, more books are ultimately returned, and the library's public relations improve.[23]

The Alameda County Library staff felt that they could have better, more positive relationships with patrons when the threat of fines was removed. Taking away fines meant taking away a potential source of patron complaints and the resulting staff defensiveness.[24] Library fines, the single controlling, punitive measure in the library's operations, loom very large in the public's perception of libraries. And it is the *positive* perception that we work so hard to foster in every detail of the work of the library.

Patsy Hansel and Robert Burgin surveyed public libraries in North Carolina on their varying overdues rates and tentatively established correlations between such factors as the fines policy, size of population, and timing of overdue notices, and these rates. While Hansel and Burgin discovered that the charging of fines had no statistically significant bearing on the overdues rate, they did notice that fine-charging libraries are likely to have more promptly returned books and that libraries that do not fine have more books eventually returned.[25]

The American Library Association's Fines and Penalties Committee could not muster any strong support for fines. Academic librarians reported that fines hardly made a difference in the return of materials; school librarians recommended the elimination of fines in the media centers; and public librarians reported that fines do not ensure prompt return, do not provide revenue beyond the costs of administering the penalties, can cause lower circulation, and unwittingly encourage book theft and mutilation.[26]

Wheeler's standard textbook on the management of public libraries points out that a few overdues are one of the costs of doing business. It is claimed that, on the average, four or five of every 100 books borrowed will be overdue, and two or three of every 10,000 borrowed never returned, no matter what the library's overdues policy is. The public library fares well when its losses are compared to the losses sustained in retail business, and is furthermore described as an exemplary guardian of public property.[27]

The decision to charge fines clearly involves a weighing of benefits and liabilities. For libraries that believe in fines, fines are associated with a higher rate of prompt return of books and therefore with more books being available for circulation when they are requested by patrons. Fines are also perceived as a good measure of control over the library operation. Libraries that have decided not to charge fines claim a higher total circulation, more books returned ultimately, and the pleasure of having a library free of penalties and free to concentrate on positive ways to build a strong and secure institution. Both points of view deserve careful consideration.

How well we know that, as one librarian wrote, "You can't lump all libraries into one pot."[28] This librarian objected to general advice proffered to the whole profession to eliminate fines. His simple advice, after realizing full success with fines, is to charge fines, by all means, if they work, but to summarily discontinue them if they do not. Whether or not fines work is in the end a judgment to be made by each circulating library.

REFERENCES

1. "Delinquent Library Patrons Face Stiff Fines and Jail," *Library Journal* 97 (May 1, 1972): 1661.

2. Robert S. Meyer Library Consulting Services, *Two Fineless Years: A History, Analysis, and Evaluation prepared for the Alameda County Library System* (Hayward, Calif., 1972), 11-12. On these pages, Meyer outlines the arguments in support of library fines.

3. "Stiff Fines at Spokane Co. Work for Washington Library," *Library Journal* 104 (February 15, 1979): 450. "Libraries Beef Up Efforts to Get Back Overdues," *Library Journal* 104 (May 1, 1979): 994. In these two reports, among others, *Library Journal* comments on the tendency of libraries to take a punitive approach towards overdues and book loss.

4. Harold J. Ettelt, "Fines and Circulation," *Library Journal* 102 (January 1, 1977): 2.

5. A. Hunter Rineer, "Law and Order in People Orientation," *American Libraries* 1 (June 1970): 528.

6. Sue Jackson, "Fines are Fine," *Library Journal* 100 (December 1, 1975): 1-83.

7. "Restoration of Fines Clicks at Sudbury, Mass.," *Library Journal* 106 (October 1, 1981): 1874-75.

8. "No-Fine Policy Flunks in Indiana," *Library Journal* 96 (May 1, 1971): 1562.

9. "Collection Agency Hired by Washington Library," *Library Journal* 102 (November 1, 1977): 2202.

10. Janice Hankins, "Fines: A Teaching Tool," *Indiana Media Journal* 2 (Winter 1980): 17-18.

11. Evelyn Geller, "Baltimore's Fine Fettle," *Library Journal* 97 (February 15, 1972): 743.

12. "Delinquent Library Patrons," 1661.

13. Rineer, 527.

14. Jean C. Pelletiere and Cheryl M. LaGuardia, "Bringing Faculty Overdues Back into the Fold," *American Libraries* 13 (April 1982): 230-231.

15. "Harvard Adopts Harsh Fines Policy," *Library Journal* 101 (July 1976): 1476.

16. "New York Delinquent Borrowers Yield to Legal Threats," *Library Journal* 103 (February 15, 1978): 2468.

17. Meyer, 12-14. The major arguments against charging fines are outlined by Meyer.

18. Ibid., 14-19.

19. Pamela Gjettum, "Overdue—Catch 025.6," *Wilson Library Bulletin* 48 (May 1974): 712.

20. Geller, 742-743.

21. John N. Berry, "Nickel Victories," *Library Journal* 100 (February 15, 1975): 351.

22. Meyer, 31.

23. Gordon S. Wade, "Special Report: Does Charging Fines Really Pay?" *Wilson Library Bulletin* 50 (October 1975): 99-100.

24. Meyer, 35.

25. Patsy Hansel and Robert Burgin, "Hard Facts about Overdues," *Library Journal* 108 (February 15, 1983): 349-350.

26. John N. Berry, "Nickel Victories—II," *Library Journal* 101 (October 15, 1976): 2105.

27. Joseph L. Wheeler, *Wheeler and Goldhor's Practical Administration of Public Libraries*, rev. by Carlton Rochell (New York: Harper & Row, 1981): 364-365.

28. Ettelt, 2.

Overdues
and the
Library's Image

Barbara Anderson

ABSTRACT. Librarians are perceived by the public as inflexible and rule-oriented; such an image discourages library use. Contributing to the image are rules such as those dealing with overdue materials. Such restrictive rules stem from an ambivalence about who the library's patrons are and from restrictive administrative structures. Since the effectiveness of strict overdues policies has been questioned, the author encourages librarians to reassess such policies. All policies and other details of the library should be consistent with attempts to encourage library use.

A photograph of a librarian that appeared recently in *People Magazine* was surprisingly reminiscent of the stern, bespectacled spinster that we conjure up in our mind's eye when we think of librarians from a past era.[1] The librarian pictured was the subject of a short article entitled "A Librarian Throws the Book at Overdue Borrowers." Interestingly enough, the article chose to spotlight the essential innocence of patrons who had been summoned to court. The Marlborough (Massachusetts) librarian, apparently oblivious to extenuating circumstances that explained the delinquence of her patrons, was just doing her job. The popular media still portray librarians as strict, inflexible guardians of book collections. It is in our role as enforcers of rules and regulations that we inspire such characterization.

When people think of libraries, they are apt to think first of our oppressive rules and regulations and our institutional atmosphere. It seems that our public image is somewhat tarnished. People feel guilty

Barbara Anderson, Head, East Winston Branch, Forsyth County Public Library, Winston-Salem, NC 27101.

when they think of libraries. Because of its demand for decorum and compliance with the letter of its regulations, the library has been compared to a church.[2] The public perception of the public library is, in some quarters, drastically different from the librarian's perception of a relevant, responsive institution. The director of the Montclair (New Jersey) Public Library asks:

> What do people think we do? Why, what they most often see us doing: charging out books, collecting petty fines and fees, compiling absurd statistics, losing our cool with teenagers, ignoring contemporary literature, and above all, enforcing restrictive rules and regulations. Some libraries actually seem to have more rules than books.[3]

Today's librarians invest heavily in strengthening community support of libraries, increasing library use, broadening services, extending to their patrons, and in all kinds of outreach efforts. Yet there is that negative perception afoot. While, on the one hand, the cheerleaders among us wave people in, library fines, many rules and regulations, and general inflexibility discourage library use.

Contributing to our image of inflexibility are, among other things, rules that prohibit the borrowing of special books, rules on what constitutes proper and sufficient application for library cards, rules requiring payment for books not returned, and penalties for lateness in returning books. It is not difficult to understand the original rationale for such rules. Our business, the free lending of books, is, after all, a unique enterprise in our communities. To stay in business we must get the books back. This has brought about a host of rules.

Our inflexibility is very much a matter of how we administer our rules just as it is obviously a matter of a preponderance of the rules themselves. In the case of books designated as "reference," there are librarians who will never permit such volumes to leave the library, and there are those who decide to weigh circumstances and permit some limited borrowing privileges. Required identification for library cards will be demanded by some staff to the letter for all applicants; by other staff, such regulations might be abridged somewhat to make new registrations possible. In the case of the patron who insists that he or she has, in fact, returned the book that our records show still charged out, one could assess the patron for the value of the book, no matter what he or she claims, or one could clear the patron's record. Surely our varying approaches make a marked difference in our patrons' satisfaction with the library. When we show even some small degree of flexibility, we win library support. In many library situations, especially where we "know" our patrons, we can judiciously relax requirements and still maintain a good degree of control. Our choice in the way we administer our policies can make as tangible a difference in our success as new registrations do, and can impart an impression of rigidity or flexibility to our patrons. In many regulated areas of the library operations, by our style of enforcement, we build or detract from positive public perceptions of the library.

Our regulations are most abundant, as one would expect, in the area of overdues. Library fines charged for overdue materials are a prominent example of library regulations. Fines are prominent to the point of being inseparable from the public's view of libraries. Patrons of libraries that have no fines often assume that they do. At the Forsyth County (North Carolina) Public Library, which has not charged fines for ten years, patrons still hesitantly return their overdue books with the understated question, "Do I owe anything?" Each time we inform an unaware patron that our Library does not charge fines, we note that the goodwill produced by this simple message is overwhelming. People do not enjoy fines any more than they enjoy being punished.

Because library fines receive so much comment in library circles, fines are a good example of our perceived inflexibility, an example on which we will focus this inquiry. The levying of fines, like any punitive approach to overdues, diverts attention from the basic cultural, educational, informational, and recreational goals of the library. Library fines, like other restrictive rules, contribute to our image of sternness and rigidity.

Contributing to libraries' general restrictiveness, fines, and, consequently, our public image is an ambivalence about who our patrons are. Libraries are ambivalent about what elements of society they are serving and even confused about how to essentially characterize society. Library policies are ostensibly fashioned to suit the characteristics of the library's particular clientele. Which of these characteristics the policy maker chooses to respond to with most emphasis is an issue that elicits opposing points of view.

Robert Meyer poses the problem of whether the library will have policies suited to considerate, rule-obeying patrons or to those who break the rules. He concluded, in the midst of his study of the Alameda County (California) Library's creation of a central overdues unit and that library's abandoning of its fines policy, that the mood of the times was for social institutions to take a more optimistic view of man's nature than they had in the past, to respond to a patron in a way that assumes he is responsible. Meyer felt that it was wrong for an institution to orient its policies to a minority rather than a majority of its patrons.[4]

On the other side of the issue, the Pennsylvania State Librarian published his view that a fines system is mandatory because of the minority who are consistently irresponsible in their library obligations. It was his belief that the basic purpose of most laws is to try to enforce on an unwilling, un-law-abiding minority conformity to some of the norms of an ordered society. He explained that the newly instituted fines policy at the State Library was aimed at patrons who were inconsiderate of the burden they placed on other library users by late return of their books.[5]

Will Manley has recently expressed the view that librarians typically "get stuck" on the negative aspects of human nature and are continually responding to the bad in the world instead of focusing on and encouraging the positive. Manley claims that by treating everyone as if untrustworthy, we set up an adversarial relationship with our patrons.[6] In other words, we mistakenly transfer "tough" reactions that may be appropriate for the irresponsible few to our whole universe of patrons and, in so doing, considerably detract from the promoting of our primary mission.

The restrictiveness of our varying policies and the staff's approach to interpreting policy, our flexibility or lack thereof, are to a large extent determined at the top. Certainly, it is often the case that a library director may insist on a solution such as fines because he was brought up in a world of fines and has a strong, subjective feeling that fines are right, proper, and necessary. A natural and predictable reaction to the problem of high overdues rates and book loss is, in this view, strictness and penalties.

Management style has an important bearing on our public image. The public can sense whether the staff is thriving or just doing the job. Maurice Marchant has concluded from his research that staff job satisfaction is the most accurate internal indicator of the public's perception of the library.[7] Additionally, Marchant has pointed out that management style is an important shaper of staff job satisfaction. He has found that a participatory style is indeed associated with a high rate of staff satisfaction and a high quality of library service.

For Marchant, "participatory" means delegating the decision making downward and, most important, trusting and listening to the staff.[8] Managers who are open and listening to staff are likely to be open and listening to patrons and to encourage that kind of posture towards patrons among staff. We conclude that management style is an important predictor of the attitudes towards library and patrons that staff communicate. Furthermore, this writer would suggest an association between openness in management style and flexibility in policies and rules.

It is through flexible, empathetic behavior that we promote a positive image of our libraries. It has been claimed that most people are "intimidated by rules and fines," put off by the library's "impersonality," and by the "officiousness of particular individuals."[9] Patron satisfaction is related in a very significant way to the librarian's talent for interpersonal relations and his or her ability to express genuineness, empathy, and respect.[10] It has been found that all professionals, including librarians, impress their clients or students or patients more by their manner of relating to their clients than by their knowledge or training.[11] But, by our inflexibility, by our punitive approach to overdues, we regularly make people feel defensive. The librarian who adopts a flexible approach lowers a patron's defenses and most effectively communicates his or her message.[12] Each staff member involved in public service launches a personal public relations program for the library. The degree of flexibility and understanding of the patron's needs that we bring to our meeting with the patron is the key to positive image-building.

The conclusions reached by the Alameda County Library staff from the "no-fines" experience would be the very conclusions one would expect from a relaxing of any punitive approach to overdues or any restrictive regulation that staff had been enforcing. The library felt that there were definitely better relations between library and patrons with no fines, that there were relations without barriers. The staff believed that patron service improved when all staff time was spent on positive activity. The staff was less defensive because there were fewer patron complaints. Everyone benefited when the emphasis on service replaced a rule-enforcing emphasis.[13] Certainly, when the public's attention is wholly diverted from the threat of penalties, the library staff appears to be involved truly in "service" rather than "control."[14]

When a library rule that seems unnecessary and oppressive to the patron is enforced, some damage is done to the patron's perception of the staff member with whom he or she has been dealing and in turn to his or her perception of the whole library. The levying and collection of a fine by a member of the library staff is a "social transaction" affecting both library and patron. Librarian and patron can relate to each other more effectively when a barrier such as the monetary penalty for late return of books is removed.[15]

While library fines contribute to our image of inflexibility, there is evidence that they do not, by any means, perfectly accomplish their intended purpose. Patsy Hansel and Robert Burgin offer sound conclusions, based on the experiences of many libraries, on the factors that affect overdues rates. Hansel and Burgin make clear that the relationship between a library's fines policy and the prompt return of materials is insignificant. In fact, they point out that although a no-fines policy may result in fewer materials being returned by the due date, it is associated with the ultimate return of more materials.[16] In other words, fines do not make a significant difference in the number of overdues and may even contribute to a higher rate of book loss.

Out of a recent effort by one of the large urban libraries to retrieve its overdue books comes evidence that fines actually stop people from returning their long-overdue books. In a glowing report on the Free Library of Philadelphia's 1983 Forgiveness Week, when the library accepted overdue materials with no fines and no questions asked, on-the-scene patron interviews revealed that fear of high fines had definitely kept patrons from returning library books they had borrowed long ago.[17]

John Berry has pointed out the absurdity of focusing so much attention on the deterrent effect fines may have on late book return, a deterrent effect that he feels is minimal. He wonders why librarians do not, instead, concern themselves with the substantial impact a fines policy has on total library use. Berry believes there is unquestionably less use of libraries because of fines. He has called fines "archaic, counter to the spirit of the Library Bill of Rights, and a vestigial remain that should be removed from librarianship."[18]

Joseph Wheeler, aware even twenty years ago of experimentation with unusually high fines as well as no fines at all, maintained that the rate of overdues (four or five for every 100 books borrowed) and the rate of book loss (two or three for every 10,000 borrowed) remain about the same no matter what our fines policy.[19]

Just as there are librarians who respond to increasing overdues rates by imposing strict regulations, there are also those who choose to relax the rules, especially in the area of penalties. In the midst of the recent steady trend toward strict penalties for overdues, we find the Sidney (Ohio) Library, for example, now has fewer overdues since it dropped fines.[20] The wide range of viewpoint and testimony should stop us from depending on fines to convey our sense of the reciprocal consideration patrons owe the library.

The intention of most library rules is to "protect the interests of all patrons," to adjust in a fair way a situation in which many people seek relatively few sources of information and recreation and to prevent any segment of the public from controlling "an information market designed for the masses."[21] However, it sometimes happens that library rules cause some people hardship and cause others to stop using the library altogether. The "aura" that surrounds an institution with all sorts of restrictive rules and regulations may even dissuade some people from ever making an initial trip to the library.

That exaggerated notion of the librarian as a "regulation-conscious wielder of datestamps" flows directly from our well-known fines for overdue materials, our many rules and regulations, and the inclination, which is surely waning, to put adherence to the letter of the regulation ahead of our broader purposes.[22] The collection of library fines, a punishing function, takes attention away from our strong service commitment to our patrons and hurts our efforts to promote the library. Our community's positive perception of the library is damaged by restrictive rules and a stern, unbending approach to their enforcement.

When we relate to our patrons in a flexible, empathetic way, in a way that assumes they are considerate and responsible, we promote the public's consideration of the library and, in fact, encourage their best behavior. Many of us will surely maintain from our library experiences that when patrons feel they are treated well by the library, they respond by fulfilling their library obligations in a responsible manner. In his explanation of the philosophy behind the Free Library's Forgiveness Week, Library Director Keith Doms openly acknowledged the "honesty and integrity" of his patrons.[23] The suspension of penalties, with this acknowledgement understood, turned out to be the ultimate strategy for motivating patrons to return public library materials.

Vital to a posture of flexibility and concern for patrons is the tone set by the library's management in its implicit and explicit encouragement to staff to administer library policies in a way that clearly announces our priorities. A reasonable degree of flexibility needs to be tacitly approved. In the interests of a positive public image, the library administration, those who manage the library's "culture," need to be good listeners to staff and patrons and strong representatives of the library's overriding values.

Consideration of whether penalties and other restrictive policies will actually work towards the library's most important goals is essential to good public relations. The effectiveness of library fines has been seriously questioned. Fines, which may be a remnant of that past era of librarianship, have been called "a testament to our pettiness and paranoia."[24] A policy such as fines for overdues would need to be reassessed to judge whether it is accomplishing enough of its intended purpose for us to tolerate its negative effects on our image. The Free Library's Forgiveness Week, which brought an outstanding 160,000 overdue books back to the library, demonstrated that dropping penalties is associated with spectacular public relations.

As far as possible, we want to align all details of the library operation with our most important message to our community. We need to free our libraries of over-strictness and an overabundance of punitive regulations. An image of rigidity conveys aloofness and detachment; an image of flexibility conveys concern for our community.

REFERENCES

1. "Trouble: A Librarian Throws the Book at Overdue Borrowers," *People* 17 (April 5, 1983): 133.

2. Will Manley, "Facing the Public," *Wilson Library Bulletin* 57 (June 1983): 846.

3. Arthur Curley, "Viewport—Service with a Snarl," *Library Journal* 97 (May 15, 1972): 1785.

4. Robert S. Meyer Library Consulting Services, *Two Fineless Years: A History, Analysis, and Evaluation prepared for the Alameda County Library System* (Hayward, Calif., 1972): 25-27.

5. A. Hunter Rineer, "Law and Order in People Orientation," *American Libraries*, 1 (June 1970): 527-528.

6. Manley, 846.

7. Maurice P. Marchant, "Participative Management, Job Satisfaction, & Service," *Library Journal* 107 (April 15, 1982): 782.

8. Marchant, 783-784.

9. Curley, 1785.

10. Manual Lopez and Richard Rubacher, "Interpersonal Psychology: Librarians and Patrons," *Catholic Library World* 40 (April 1969): 484-485.

11. Ric Calabrese, "Interaction Skills and the Librarian," *Illinois Libraries* 55 (January 1973): 9.

12. Ibid.

13. Meyer, 35-39.

14. Curley, 1785.

15. Meyer, 35.

16. Patsy Hansel and Robert Burgin, "Hard Facts about Overdues," *Library Journal* 108 (February 15, 1983): 349-350.

17. Art Milner, "Forgiveness Week," *Library Journal* 109 (April 1, 1984): 630.

18. John N. Berry, "Nickel Victories," *Library Journal* 100 (February 15, 1975): 351.

19. Joseph L. Wheeler and Herbert Goldhor, *Practical Administration of Public Libraries* (New York: Harper & Row, 1962): 307.

20. "Free Coffee and No Fines in Sidney, Ohio," *Library Hotline* 13 (January 9, 1984): 4.

21. Sam Clay, "To Fine or Not to Fine," *Virginia Librarian* 18 (Summer 1971): 32.

22. Milo Nelson supplies the quotation in "Miss Piggy Unjustly Upbraided," *Wilson Library Bulletin* 55 (June 1981): 724.

23. Milner, 627.

24. Curley, 1785.

Overdues:
A Bibliography

Terry Bossley

I. TO FINE OR NOT TO FINE

1. Berry, John. "Nickel Victories." *Library Journal* 100 (February 15, 1975): 351.

   Editorial: Berry agrees that a national policy or position on the question of library fines should be developed. He also argues that fines often have the opposite effect from the one intended—to ensure the return of books so that they will be accessible to others.

2. Berry, John. "Nickel Victories—II." *Library Journal* 101 (October 15, 1976): 2105.

   Again, editorial opinion of Berry that supports his statements in February, and once again shows the wide differences in the administrative point of view about fines from one library to another.

3. Bryant, Helen. "Fines? No. Encourage Use, Eliminate Fines." *Indiana Media Journal* 2(Winter 1980): 16, 18.

   Self-explanatory article about the positive effects of no fines in a school situation.

4. Clay, Sam. "To Fine or Not to Fine." *Virginia Librarian* 17 (Summer 1971): 32.

5. "Delinquent ILL Borrowers Face 50-cents-a-day Fines." *American Libraries* 14 (April 1983): 176.

6. Ettelt, Harold J. "Fines and Circulation." *Library Journal* 102 (January 1, 1977): 2.

   A community college where a fine-free policy was quite positive, resulting in double circulation for students and significantly increased use by faculty. This library employed a no-lend policy (if you're overdue, you cannot borrow more materials).

Terry Bossley, Librarian, Perquimans County Library, Hertford, NC 27944.

7. Geller, Evelyn. "Baltimore's Fine Fettle." *Library Journal* 97 (February 15, 1972): 743.

8. Hankins, Janice. "Fines: A Teaching Tool." *Indiana Media Journal* 2 (Winter 1980): 17-18.

Explains the use of fines as a teaching tool in elementary school media centers.

9. "Hearing Invokes Magic to Make Fines Vanish—The Magic Alternatives." *American Libraries* 7 (September 1976): 504.

An article about a special ALA-sponsored hearing on fines and penalties, including lively reaction to written statements on professional attitudes towards this aspect of library management.

10. Howard, Edward N. "Breaking the Fine Barrier." *ALA Bulletin* 63 (December 1969): 1541.

11. Jackson, Sue. "Fines are Fine." *Library Journal* 100 (December 1, 1975): 2184.

This public library experiment with a fine-free policy for six months ended as a failure. The library implemented a modified fines policy, and the percentage of overdues dropped.

12. "Restoration of Fines Clicks at Sudbury, Mass." *Library Journal* 106 (October 1, 1981): 1874-1875.

Profiles a situation in which a no-fines policy did not work. Materials returned dropped from 96 percent to 80 percent after the no-fines policy was instituted. Notes that more and more items were being kept out longer, and more and more overdue notices were being sent.

13. "Stiff Fines at Spokane County Work for Washington Library." *Library Journal* 104 (February 15, 1979): 450.

Implementation of tougher fines policies bring about a significant drop in overdues.

14. Truett, Carol. "To Fine or Not to Fine: One School Library's Experience." *Top of the News* 37 (Spring 1981): 277-280.

A school library initiated a no-fines policy with great success. A chart is included in the article for comparing the loss of books before and after implementation of the policy. Benefits of the no-fines policy are noted.

15. Wade, Gordon S. "Special Report: Does Charging Fines Really Pay?" *Wilson Library Bulletin* 50 (October 1975): 99-100, 175.

This account looks at a one-year study of the effects of fines, compared with a no-fines policy; focusing specifically on the effects of fines upon the return of books and other library materials. Based on that study, the library's desire to reduce clerical tasks, and public relations, fines were abolished.

II. TRICKS OF THE TRADE

1. "Action Exchange." *American Libraries* 11 (December 1980): 650.
Libraries have tried many ploys to get patrons to return overdue materials—even overdue notices with a light touch.

2. "Boy Scout Retrieves Overdues." *American Libraries* 12 (September 1981): 471.
The Scouts, as a community service project, sent notices to delinquent patrons notifying them that the materials would be picked up. With Boy Scout help, 334 overdues were retrieved.

3. "Burgers for Overdues." *Library Journal* 105 (March 15, 1980): 669.
New York's Geneva Free Library and the community's Burger King franchise teamed up in a successful drive to recover overdues.

4. Cain, Carolyn, "A New Look at Overdue Problems." *School Library Journal* 28 (November 1981): 45.
A high school media center used a simple process of involving all the parties affected by the overdue problem in helping to reach a solution. Step-by-step methods are laid out.

5. "Chicago Public Gets Tough with Delinquent Patrons." *Library Journal* 104 (December 1, 1979): 2504.
Stiffer fines (changed from $10 to $50 to $500 per item), going through the legal motions necessary to have arrest warrants served on the worst offenders, and making it harder for new borrowers to get a library card are all reported as efforts by the Chicago Public Library to get tougher on overdues.

6. "Conscience Days for Public Libraries." *Library Journal* 57 (December 1, 1932): 1008.

7. "D.C. Fine-Free Week Brings Back 18,000." *Library Journal* 105 (October 15, 1980): 2146.
A D.C. library launched a broad-gauge publicity campaign to prod people to return books during fine-free week.

8. "$500 Fines at Chicago Public Library." *Library Journal* 104 (August 1979): 1510.

Same information as "Chicago Public Gets Tough with Delinquent Patrons." (See no. 5.)

9. Guyatt, Joy. "Points and the Implementation of an Overdue Policy." *Australian Academic and Research Libraries* 10 (September 1979): 179-184.

This account focuses on an undergraduate library whose loan regulations are strictly administered along with a point system. Flowcharts are used to show the overdue procedure.

10. "Librarians Meet to Fight Book Thieves." *American Libraries* 16 (November 1983): 648.

11. "Libraries Beef-Up Efforts to Get Back Overdues." *Library Journal* 104 (March 15, 1980): 668.

Article reports that libraries are trying tougher tactics on their efforts to get people to return overdue library materials. Among the strategies that seem to be working: mail-grams and the threat of legal action.

12. Manley, Will. "Facing the Public." *Wilson Library Bulletin* 57 (June 1983): 846-847.

Argues that the cause of the problem of overdues is the library's attitude in dealing with delinquent borrowers. Notes that the Scottsdale Public Library has a "Customer Service" department for handling overdues; this approach accentuates the positive and treats patrons as very important people.

13. "Mayor Himself Gets Books Back to Baltimore Library." *American Libraries* 13 (October 1982): 562-563.

As part of a "bring back the book—make yourself feel good" campaign, city agencies, businesses, and professional groups volunteered to telephone delinquent borrowers. The mayor of Baltimore was one of the local celebrities who participated—58 percent of the "unable-to-collects" were brought back.

14. "Mediation Center Solves Problem of Overdues." *American Libraries* 14 (April 1983): 176.

Orange County Public Library in Hillsborough, NC, rejected the idea of small claims court because of high case fees and negative publicity. A new strategy had delinquent borrowers come before the local center's volunteer mediators.

15. Nelson, W.D. "Rooting for the Home Team Brings Returns." *Wilson Library Bulletin* 57 (October 1982): 143.

In a cooperative program with the Baltimore Orioles, baseball fans returned overdue library books to get a discount on tickets to the ball park.

16. "Newark's Overdue Book Week." *Library Journal* 57 (May 1, 1932): 438.

17. "No Fines and Tall Tales." *Library Journal* 104 (June 1, 1979): 1207.

Cumberland County Public Library, in North Carolina, declared a fine-free week during National Library Week and also a "tall-tale" contest for the most creative excuse for an overdue.

18. Pelletiere, J.C., and LaGuardia, C.M. "Bringing Faculty Overdues Back into the Fold." *American Libraries* 13 (April 1982): 230-231.

19. Peterson, Nancy H. "Upping the Ante on Overdues." *Library and Archival Security* 3 (Spring 1980): 25-27.

The Knoxville-Knox County Public Library (Tenn.) used the Western Union Mailgram to recover long overdue materials. After this system proved effective, a mailgram terminal was installed in the main library on a limited contract basis. The terminal is simple to operate and requires a standard telephone for immediate access to the main computer via a toll-free number.

20. "Saint Paul Hits Delinquents with Service Charges." *Library Journal* 106 (February 15, 1981): 404.

This library decided to scrap fines and levy "service charges" on delinquent borrowers who do not return items after a four-week loan period and a five-day grace period. Goals of the system include providing a stronger incentive for returning books and holding the patron responsible for the expense of sending overdue notices. The service charges are listed.

III. COLLECTION AGENCIES

1. "Collection Agency Hired by Washington Library." *Library Journal* 102 (November 1, 1977): 2202.

With distressing annual losses in stolen and overdue books, the King County Library system decided to "get tough," doubling penalties for overdues and hiring a local collection agency to go after delinquent borrowers owing more than $15. Comparative statistics are shown.

2. Mitchell, W. Bede. "Retrieving Overdues Through a Collection Agency: One Academic Library's Approach." *Library Journal* 108 (November 1, 1983): 2030-2031.

A thorough study of retrieving overdues through a collection agency, specifically detailing the action and results of the collection system. The system proved very effective for this academic library, and it would appear to be workable in other types of libraries.

3. "Only One Overdue Notice." *Unabashed Librarian* 42 (1982): 6.

A new policy for the Salt Lake County Library System is outlined: to save postage and staff time, the only overdue notice sent would be a bill mailed to the patron's house. Any uncollected accounts amounting to twenty dollars or more were submitted to a collection agency.

4. "Philadelphia Using Collection Agency." *Wilson Library Bulletin* 56 (May 1982): 654-655.

Philadelphia's six-month experiment in making use of a commercial collection agency is reported as successful. As a result, the library planned to turn delinquent accounts over to a collection agency selected on a bid basis. The method of the collection agency and the approximate cost are included in the article.

IV. LEGAL ACTION

1. Batchelder, Muriel. "Retrieving Books Through Small Claims Court." *Library Journal* (February 1, 1952): 181-182.

Examines the use of the law in retrieving materials through small claims court. The article advises librarians to discuss the total problem with a judge and stresses the use of court action as the last resort and the need to educate public opinion. Argues that court action is necessitated by the irresponsible citizen who disregards the rights of others.

2. "Delinquent Library Patrons Face Stiff Fines and Jail." *Library Journal* 97 (May 1, 1972): 1661.

Armed with statistics of the value of books not returned and thoroughly researching the legal aspects of the issue, the Director of City Libraries in Memphis, Tennessee, convinced the City Council of the need for a new city ordinance. Now anyone who fails to return public library books can spend up to 30 days in jail and be fined $50.

3. Dumenil, R. "Defaulters." *Library Assistant* 12 (1915): 12.

4. Eisner, Joseph. "Recovery by Court Action." *Wilson Library Bulletin* 37 (February 1963): 485-486.

Shows the effective and successful use of court action to recover long overdue materials in Nassau County, New York. Outlines the procedures for a library to follow through court. Claims that warning letters from an attorney and a subpoena from the court evoke a response unmatched by other methods, ensuring "95 percent recovery of materials with maximum public relations value for the library."

5. "A Librarian Throws the Book at Overdue Borrowers." *People* 17 (April 5, 1982): 133.

Describes the crackdown on overdue borrowers in a Massachusetts library for the "willful detention of library books." Two hundred residents faced their first criminal charge as the library tried to recover materials.

6. "Man Jailed for Library Fines." *Unabashed Librarian* 30 (1979): 27.

Another example of the library feeling compelled to pursue one of its worst violators of the return policy. The patron was convicted of willfully holding library books, a misdemeanor (90 days in jail).

7. Stetson, W.K. "Delinquent Borrowers." *Library Journal* 14 (1889): 403-404.

Written nearly 100 years ago, this article gives examples of using the legal system to stimulate the return of materials. Bridgeport, Conn., used the practice of sending a copy of a municipal ordinance imposing a $10 fine for failure to return books. In actual practice the aid of the police was rarely used. Gives a little historical perspective to the overdues problem.

8. Vale, G.F. "On the Track of the Defaulter." *Library Assistant* 5 (1907): 251-252.

9. Van Oosbree, Charlyne. "Book 'Em! or Case of the Missing Book." *Unabashed Librarian* 40 (1981): 15-16.

10. "Woman Sues After Arrest for Overdue Book." *Library Journal* 108 (July 1983): 1298.

An account of a "delinquent" patron who was arrested and jailed briefly only to find out the library system was in error. The patron sued for damages.

V. STUDIES

1. "Dunning Doesn't Pay in Collecting Fines." *American Libraries* 12 (October 1981): 517.

Reports that Cleveland (Ohio) Public Library found that sending overdue notices had no effect on fines collected.

2. Goehlert, Robert. "The Effect of Loan Policies on Circulation Recalls." *Journal of Academic Librarianship* 5 (May 1979): 80.

3. Hansel, Patsy and Robert Burgin. "Hard Facts About Overdues." *Library Journal* 108 (February 15, 1983): 349-350.

A study of public libraries in NC to compile data to determine which of the tactics used in the war against overdues were most effective. Includes tables.

4. Lyons, A.G. "Circulation Policies, Overdues, and Fines: Results of a Survey of Academic Health Science Libraries." chart *Medical Library Association Bulletin* 69 (July 1981): 326-329.

5. "Overdue Study." *Unabashed Librarian* 33 (1979): 3.

Looks at different circulation loan periods to trace when materials were returned.

VI. GENERAL

1. Curley, Arthur. "Viewpoint—Service with a Snarl." Library Journal 97 (May 15, 1972): 1785.

2. Gjettum, Pamela. "Catch—025.6." *Wilson Library Bulletin* 48 (May 1974): 711-712.

The Catch—025.6 is that revitalizing outreach (taking books to trailer parks, etc.) can have a deleterious effect on circulation control.

3. Willis, Tony. "Overdue." *New Library World* 83 (March 1982): 41.

A tongue-in-cheek comment about the way the media reported the return of a lost book.

Index